The Art of Lo

G000138014

Bringing c

Gary. G McFarlane

A self-help guide to improve all aspects of relationships whether married or single and includes therapist's active techniques and Cognitive Behavioural principles, drawing upon Gary's learning's from Psychodynamic and Systemic principles and life experiences as a Husband, Father, Christian, Solicitor, Mediator, Relationship counsellor, Sex Therapist and Sex Addiction Therapist.

Registered: Mon Nov 15 23:06:36 UTC 2010

Title: Relationships & Relationship: Love Don't Live Here any More

Fingerprint:
8ee447a82c340b660537128c98f4567e0fcfd96516c3b0ad
a70636fb22c02692

MCN: C22VP-56

Dedication

To the individuals and couples whom I have been privileged to counsel over many years and have provided the knowledge and experience which I now pass on so that you and others may benefit from their journey.

To my sister Shirley.

Table of contents

Acknowledgments

I wish to recognise and honour my family who provided the loving support during a particularly turbulent and life change period of 5 years of my life. Always there for me.

In particular I return love and appreciation to my soul mate, pillow companion and wife – Cynthy; my children Pierce and Mia-Claire – who are my pride and joy and my mother who brought me into this world and gave to me the foundational qualities which have served me well throughout life.

To the one God who made me – Lord of Heaven and Earth.

Introduction

What do you do and what happens, when your whole world – as you know it – comes toppling down? All the foundations deemed important by society, such as career, professionalism, relationship, finance, children, house, health, life style and quality of life, are shaken to the core. Maybe it has not gone that far for you, but certainly life has some pain and it often comes from relationship conflicts. This stuff of relationships is proving more problematic than ever thought. It seems to work for others. Why didn't the formula work? Maybe it did. Maybe it does. Was application at fault?

Pain hurts. But the journey toward change and destiny begins in the midst of pain. If you can change your mind – because of increased understanding – then you can change your life!

Some people remain single because they are frightened of commitment or change. Commitment may mean a different thing to each person. They may use lack of closeness and a single life style to regulate and control levels of intimacy. Yet there is a deep cry inside to be in relationship with someone. If you are not currently in a couple relationship, here are some tools for later application. Learn them well now. Your turn may be coming when some of the material may serve you well.

In this book are some words of wisdom which, applied diligently, have the potential to transform your relationships.

Do nothing and something will be done to you – for sure.

"Would you tell me, which way I ought to go from here?"

"That depends a good deal on where you want to get to", said the cat.

"I don't much care", said Alice.

"Then it doesn't matter which way you go", said the cat

"As long as I get somewhere."

Alice added as an explanation

"Oh, you're sure to do that." said the cat

"If you only walk long enough"

Alice felt that this could not be denied".

(Lewis Carroll, Alice in Wonderland)

Chapter 1

First thing first

"It isn't that they can't see the solution. It is that they can't see the problem." — <u>G.K. Chesterton</u>.

Here is a challenge. Which of these four kinds of person best represent you and your current frame of mind concerning the issues you are facing?

- You will read this book, but are not really ready to digest all that is demonstrated and so within a few days very little has been retained or remembered because it never really went into the mind; or

- You read and agree with most or what you hear, but like so many other aspects of your life this is yet another trophy to be hung in your mind for just a short while and you do nothing with the information. It is stored in the recesses of your mind with lots and lots of other teachings that you have had; or

- You read and have good intentions, but maybe the words are too challenging and require too much from you. It may require you to change. Over ensuing days and weeks you begin to rationalise what was said and compare it to other teachings or knowledge that you have. As you ponder the things you have heard, they gradually become jumbled and mixed up with other teachings. The words are stifled by what you thought you knew. The content is forgotten because it needed action and you are not yet willing to take action; or

- You read, assess and digest. Since you have truly listened and have a mindset motivation and desire for change, seeds of humility, humbleness and purpose are tools which create your focus for change.

I challenge you to consider where you are in your thoughts, expectations and motivation as you read this book. Think about where you are at as you commence reading this book. Which one of those descriptions best represents the extent of your motivation? Don't be too hard on yourself! Rather, be honest. You see, knowing where you are at is a first step towards change.

Chapter 2

Masks and games people play

Things are not always as they appear to be! The facades soon enough come tumbling down because one cannot keep up appearances for long.

Most of us have a "true" and a "false" self. When we do not much like our self, our relationship with others will be affected. We will try to portray a side to others intended to make them want to like us even if we are probably portraying a false self. We think that if others see our true self they will not like us. Many of us do have a problem with our self. We do not like our self very much. We would not go out with our self if we had the choice.

It is self-evident that childhood experiences must have a profound formative effect upon the beliefs we have about ourselves and upon our expectations of others. Most of us fail to take those childhood experiences into account when we run into trouble later on in life. So much of the past continues to live in the present and affect the future. Those important carers (usually mother and father) leave us with good and not so good, first impressions of relationships, which at some point no longer work for us. The adult needs to find a new way.

We were made to be in relationships. If you doubt it look at our expanding singleness status and singleness occupancies. Yet there is a massive growth in the mobile phone industry as we need to be in touch with others. But relationships go wrong. Conflicts arise. Some conflicts in relationship can be seen as an attempt to put right experiences which have gone wrong in the past. Relationships are so often the place of healing of past hurts from the stuff of our young growing up years, which affected the way we do relationships.

Let's focus on the couple, but always recognize that you are a unique individual within the couple and the couple is within a household and the household is a part of the wider extended family and the family a part of the family tree of descendants. As a couple you function, not in isolation as an island, but as part of wider systems of interactions. That is important, because the pull and influence of those systems can be very powerful and strong. Ignorance of that can be disastrous. In-laws can have their far reaching tentacles in the couple relationship in very subtle ways.

Often, the answer to loneliness is only partly met by people. Some people say that falling in love is involuntary. I am not sure about that. What I am sure about is that being in love and remaining in love is very much a matter of your choice.

Coasting in the relationship whilst waiting for an event (perhaps the children leaving school or some other unacknowledged and unconscious event), means that, for sure, you are probably in a relationship that is going down hill!

In a survey of family lawyers in 2004, extra-marital affairs were found to be the main reason for UK divorces. Adultery was the major factor and led to 27% of divorces, followed by family strains at 18%, emotional and physical abuse at 17%, mid-life crisis at 13%, workaholicism at 6% and other addictions, such as alcohol and gambling as at 6%. Sexuality, the expression of our sexuality, sex addiction, particularly internet pornography and cybersex is challenging all of those statistics. Adultery, an affair or one night stand, is no longer to be assumed as taking place with a real third person. Cybersex, our love affair with the internet and such gadgets, means that the third person is now a third "thing" with tentacles in the relationship – but not a real person who fights fair and with whom we can fight!

Shaped by circumstances from birth

Picture the new born baby which starts life with innocence and a brain with few impressions. It starts to experience life and living and soon the brain has some impressions and grooves being carved into it. Good and not so good experiences and impressions. A distorted image develops.

The individual distorted image of a male coming with his own unique impressions and experiences of life and the individual distorted image of a female also coming with her own unique impressions and experiences of life, get together (perhaps marry) and become an item. The two distorted images are suppose to live a lifetime together in harmony. Their differing impressions and experiences of life, including the adaptations they have had to make to survive life, may no longer serve them well in the new twosome. Adapt and survive or live with conflict is now the choice. The two individuals look sound from external appearances, but inside they have many unresolved issues.

Change may cost and you may not be wanting, willing or ready for change. In truth others can try to stimulate us into action, but a level of own motivation is necessary. Some Motivational interviewing work from a therapist may be beneficial. Putting this book down for a while until then, may be a good move!

Chapter 3

Pain hurts

"To have a right to do a thing is not at all the same as to be right in doing it." — <u>G.K. Chesterton</u>

Marital fit with Pinch & Crunch

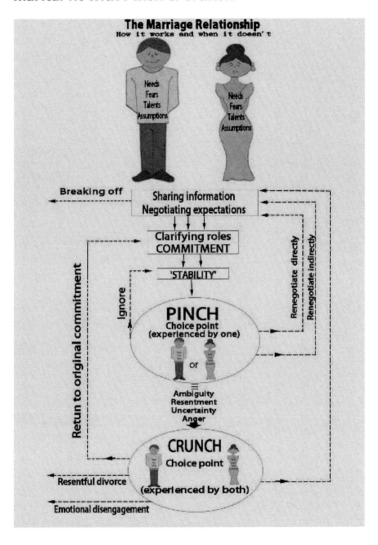

Diagram: Pinch & Crunch

We enter relationships at the courting stage, bringing with us all our stuff (good and not so good). We are actually negotiating with each other as we adapt and seek to ascertain

15

whether there are enough common attractions that can hold and carry the relationship. There is a collusive fit which brought us together, but that is not enough to keep us in courtship.

If time proves to be a glue, then time may also see the relationship develop to permanency or marriage. A pinch will disrupt harmony and we must decide which option to take to deal with the pinch which has the potential to de-stabilise. Options include fight, flight, separate, divorce, counselling or going back to an earlier stage in the relationship and starting again to renegotiate needs and expectations.

Crunches are an even more painful and de-stabilising assaults on the relationship and like pinches, we must choose an option, including doing nothing. Doing nothing is to coast in the relationship. We are then at the mercy of an event in the future which will occur and take the choice out of our hands, so that outcomes are no longer determinable by the parties.

Henry Dicks says: *"The partner attracts because he or she represents or promises a rediscovery of an early lost aspect of the subjects own personality which owing to an early conditioning has been recast as an object for attack or denial"*.

We get a glimpse of that from the person who was the life and soul of the party, who attracted everyone's attention, including yours. You were overwhelmed when they gravitated to you – a shy and introverted person. Your attraction to them is very much their life of the party spirit. Years later when the two have been together for some time, those very same qualities start to gripe and annoy. Those same qualities are now viewed as showing off (not life of the party). They are now seen as attention seeking and embarrassing! Why? What has changed? The person has not changed or have they?

The fact is we fall in love with the person that has sufficient degrees of difference and similarities which complement us and then we spend a lifetime trying to change them and make them more like us. The very things that attracted us to them become the very same things that we start to dislike and try to change.

Could it be that we never did reach a point of accepting them unconditionally for who they were, but in fact it was conditional, with the intent of changing them over time. Robin Skynner says: *"Relationship is always an attempt at growth and healing oneself and finding oneself again, however disastrously. Any attempt may fail for lack of sufficient understanding or external help"*. Don't dismiss too readily what Dicks and Skynner say. There may be something in it.

If you can change your mind, you can change your life. Your mind is your greatest limiter and inhibiter. Don't store up good for tomorrow what you could do today. Be aware of the inhibiters and allies in your life.

Chapter 4

Unconscious needs which influence the journey – some tools

Know the person and the opponent with whom you are in conflict. Let's look at some useful self help tools for improving conflicts in relationships.

Core Emotional Needs

Be aware of your top 10 core emotional needs, but even more importantly, be very sure that you know your top 3 core emotional needs. The very fact that we are human, means that we have these 10 core emotional needs, which have to be met. When life and circumstances do not keep these needs topped up and some dwindle beyond our critical level, then we will react, often unconsciously. Fight or flight will soon demand attention when our core emotional needs are not being met.

Fight can take the form of creating conflicts, but not being aware that we are being more contentious than usual! Flight means that we move away from a situation, into a place where we think our needs will be better met. That can take the form of longer hours at work because work or the people in the work place bring a form of comfort. They are danger zones unless we beginning to read the signs.

Our partner plays a part in meeting our core emotional needs, but they are not responsible. They cannot meet all of those needs. All of the systems within which we interact (such as work, home life, social, sports etc) play a part in meeting those needs, not one person only.

Which are your top 3 needs? Is it *Acceptance, Affection, Appreciation, Approval, Attention, Comfort, Encouragement, Respect, Security or Support?*

Many women can identify with the need for Security within their top 3 and many men include Respect.

When you have ranked your top 3, try ranking your partner's top 3. Then have a discussion. What you do not know, then you cannot affect or do much about. What you know about and can see, then you can affect for good – or chose not to – but you now have choice!

Core Values

Be aware of your core values. If our core values are trampled, de-valued or undermined, then we may fight and do battle (out of character sometimes) and even take ourselves by surprise! There are some values we will not give up - at least not without a furious fight, but we and our partner may not recognise what is happening.

Values are caught and not taught. They are a part of who we are and do not change very easily, no matter how persuasive is the influence. It takes time to reconsider, process, assess and change values. Undermine someone's values at your own risk!

These are some values: **Technical excellence, Accomplishment, Competence, Contentment, Creativity, Culture, Economic Security, Enjoyment, Esteem, Fitness, Freedom/Flexibility, Friendship, Integrity, Personal growth, Popularity, Power, Faith, Security, Self Confidence, Status, Strong Convictions, Taking Risks, Uniqueness, Wealth, Winning, Experience, Teamwork, Perfectionism, Stability, Honesty, Construction,** (and any other you wish to name).

Chose your top 5. Turn a blank A4 piece of paper landscape and fold it in a concertina way, in 5 equal columns. Write each of your top 5 (one per column) at the top of each column. Have a dustbin nearby. Decide which word you would be willing to give up and live without. Tear that strip off which contains that word. Tear it into little pieces and throw it in the bin. (Don't just screw it up. You might be tempted to reclaim in from the bin!). Once gone, it is gone.

How does it feel to have to live life without that value?

Now tear off a second one and keep repeating the exercise, giving thought to what you have done after disposing of each one. Do so until you are left with just one value.

How do you feel? Can you empathise with another person who feels like their values have been trashed time and time again? What does it make you want to do?

Stubborn as a Mule!

We can become as stubborn as a Mule! We pull against each other to achieve our purpose and refuse to exercise anything like a more conciliatory approach, especially when we feel hurt or got at. So often there is a better way to achieve win/win, if we only take time out to stop and think. Yet for long periods we fall into roles and role expectations. We pull and push against each other, when in fact we are after the very same thing. Perhaps we were seeking to get a core emotional need met.

Jake and Jasmine

Jake and Jasmine are close and balanced. Life experiences and life stages, with the differing developmental changes each will go through in life, will challenge the relationship. It happens to all relationships.

For a period of time we try to regain balance and closeness in the relationship through

24

repeated attempts and thought out strategies - like Jake & Jasmine.

JAKE AND JASMINE

We were close and the relationship was balanced.

JAKE AND JASMINE

Life stages and stuff caused Jake to move.

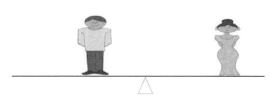

Feeling rejected, Jasmine reacts by moving away.

They ended up being distant with each other, but balanced!

Life can continue to work like this reasonably well, even though you both know that it is not how you like it or want it. Close observation will depict a couple who are actually balanced – on the see-saw of life, but there is distance between them. (That is very different to the closeness and balance they first had (seen in the first diagram of them above). The problem is that over time, something will happen to affect the relationship and take choice out of both of their hands and control.

Be in control of change or change will be done to you.

Neither like the distance between them, but they do not know what to do. So eventually Jasmine reasoned things out and resolved that something must be done to break the status quo and so swallowed her pride and went across to Jake. They were very much out of balance and could not remain like that for long. She felt she had given too much and Jake had not met her half way and so soon scurried back to her end.

JAKE AND JASMINE

After a period of time at their separate ends, with distance between them, Jake resolved to do something to mend the rift. It was his turn to try. He swallowed his pride and went across to be with Jake. The problem is that

27

it never felt fair to him. They were very much out of balance and could not remain like that for long. He felt that he had given too much and Jasmine had now not met him half way. He soon scurried back to his end. They were both exhausted, but still separate and distant.

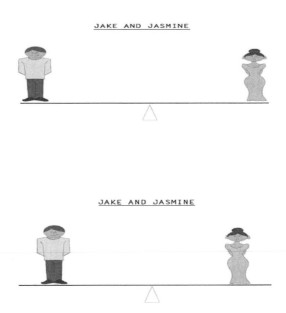

JAKE AND JASMINE

JAKE AND JASMINE

They worked out that each could give a bit. (Just like the mules, give and take could achieve mutual benefit). Giving a bit each at a time, eventually drew them closer together in a balanced way and met both of their needs.

JAKE AND JASMINE

JAKE AND JASMINE

Eventually they got back closeness. There is probably little point asking why they had moved in the first place! I guess that is how life is! Stuff happens which pushes relationships apart. The very important point is that they are close again and that is what counts! Learn from the experience.

Trust issues

When trust has gone, it is **Time** which becomes the healer. It needs action. Doing positive things as you live life together builds positive experience, which with time, begins to replace those negative experiences. We need to use the "Emotional Bank Account" model of making more deposits and fewer withdrawals, to re-built goodwill. Goodwill is what sees us through the rocky and turbulent times.

Emotional Bank Account

The same principle applies to that of using our Bank accounts. The relationship is an account. We need to make more deposits into it than withdrawals. Deposits are things that re-build trust and endear us to our partner. We shall look later at how to do that with tools such as the **Happy day exercises** and **a Sexy surprise**. Withdrawals are those things which decrease trust and take out of the relationship.

Get a plan of action

The Four Square diagram is an action plan that helps us to take first steps. Don't focus on the end or how much needs to be done. Focus again on just taking first steps, but ensure your plan is "SMART" ie Specific, Measurable, Achievable, Realistic & Time-bounded.

The questions to ask in this order are:

1. Where are we now?   2.Where do we want to be?

3. What is stopping us? 4. What is the first step?

FOUR SQUARE DIAGRAM

1. Where are we now?	2. Where do we want to be?
3. What is stopping us?	**4. What is the first step?**

S=specific M=measurable A=achievable R=realistic T=time bonded

Each of you should have a copy of the sheet. Individually write at least 3 answers to each question in the 4 boxes. Then together discuss each of your answers.

Chapter 5

Not ready yet!

Changing your mind to change your life for better (1)

"It isn't that they can't see the solution. It is that they can't see the problem." — G.K. Chesterton

Some behaviours are entrenched and deep rooted so that they need more intensive work in an individual in order to effect beneficial change in the couple relationship. Often there are truly addictive behaviours which are quite problematic.

What if you are not at a place where you can start using the tools and the journey towards healing of the relationship? They may not yet be wanted or a willingness to even pick them up and use them!

If you can change your mind, you can absolutely change your life. So let's begin a journey of changing your mind; but before then, let's look at your heart. It is a heart thing! Then the mind follows and action is the command from the mind to act in a particular way.

Some Cognitive Behavioural Principles (CBT)

The way in which humans learn and adapt their behaviour is a source of constant investigation. Observing animal behaviour has been useful. Pavlov investigated the salivation response of dogs and coined a phrase known as classical conditioning. I shall return to this later on.

Thorndike investigated the attempts of cats to get out of a box and demonstrated that the cat could learn and remember and repeat the same action again.

Whilst habit is a constant companion, when we speak about it, we tend to do so with negative connotations. In other words habits tend to be viewed as negative. In fact habits come to our aid every day of our waking life. Without them, the brain might overload as it tries to act out our requirements. Think about the journey to work. So frequently when we look back we realise we went through the traffic lights when they were green and stopped when it was red. If we walked, we probably took a familiar route. We did not need to concentrate on the route. Our body and brain just took us there. Habit can therefore be helpful. There are, however, some habits that we recognise to be unhelpful and even quite destructive.

We all need to continue learning. Learning can change habits. Learning is defined as "a change in behaviour which occurs as a result of previous experience".

Concentrating on behaviour alone can be successful. In other words, concentrating on changing behaviour is helpful. What we now know, however, is that taking thoughts and feelings (cognitions) into account, alongside behaviour, can be even more beneficial.

Our belief can be the very thing that stops us achieving desired change. Challenging our belief (cognitions), by supplying new information on which to base new learning – can effect change.

Challenging the evidence for a particular belief may show the belief to have no proper foundation and result in revised thinking. That is called cognitive restructuring. Cognitive restructuring (by challenging a particular belief) alongside behavioural change can be more effective in effecting change.

Cognitive behavioural therapy is about what a person actually does (their actions), as well as their thoughts, feelings and beliefs about those behaviours. The thoughts, beliefs and feelings are the cognitions.

1. Behaviours

Predisposing factors: there are some general upbringing experiences (from childhood), which include cultural, social, religious norms and the attitudes and beliefs those experiences create. Also, each of us has particular personality traits.

A particular behaviour that we have observed can predispose us (set down a script in our minds) that cause us to behave in that particular way. The behaviour predisposes us to behave in that way.

Example: when we were young and television was turned off whenever there was a couple becoming amorous, may have left us with an impression that there is something embarrassing about kissing and sex.

2. Precipitating factors

There may be experiences, events or expectations that we have - before a particular behaviour is displayed. It may now be set down as a script in our mind so that when we experience those particular events and expectations, then a particular type of behaviour will want to take place. The smell of alcohol may have created feelings of anxiety because past experience is that the smell of alcohol on a father meant grief for the whole household.

3. Maintaining factors

The consequences of a particular behaviour may mean that the behaviour is more likely to be repeated.

A raised voice whilst a parent was trying to help with homework when we were young may have caused tears. Our partner's attempts to explain something to us which we do not understand may evoke the same reaction in us as the parent experience. We may react to our partner in a very uncharacteristic way because we are influenced by a past way of behaving which has been maintained.

CBT does not seek to predict a course of action before it occurs. It is a tool for making sense of what has already happened. When the behaviour is properly understood, it will involve identifying the predisposing, precipitating or maintaining factors that gave rise to the consequences of the behaviour.

During this learning, we can change our cognitions and thus affect the behaviour for the future. Pavlov experimented with dogs by putting out food and then ringing a bell. What he found was that the hungry dog had observable salivary response to the anticipated food when the dog heard a bell ring summonsing it for food. It anticipated being fed. The ringing of the bell was a conditioned stimulus. The stimulus is paired with the ringing of the bell and being given food, which caused the salivary glands to secrete saliva in anticipation.

During the experiment Pavlov then changed the method. He started to ring the bell frequently and the dog arrived initially with the salivary response expecting food, but there was no food. After a while the salivary response died away because the dog no longer expected to find food waiting.

The pairing was broken. In other words the ringing of the bell equals food. In anticipation of the food there was a salivary gland response.   When the pairing was broken the response also changed.

We have all learned inappropriate pairings and associations which have predisposed us, precipitated and caused us to maintain certain types of behaviours. If we can learn more about those predisposing, precipitating and maintaining factors, we are some way towards changing our cognition. As we change our cognition (the way we think, feel and believe), then we start to change our behaviour. In other words, as we change our mind (our cognition) we can change our life (because we start to change our behaviours as well). What we think is who we are.

Where the mind is the heart will follow. Changing what the mind thinks will also change what the heart follows.

Recognise that if a stimuli has been present for a long time and a behaviour follows, constant repetition means reinforcement has been taking place over the years and habit has set in. Habit is not just something we do. It is based on stimuli that create automatic thoughts, beliefs, feelings and then behaviours. (These are the traits and hallmarks of a potential addiction).

If a stimuli is removed from a particular situation that can also increase the likelihood of a behaviour occurring. In other words behaviours can have positive reinforcement or negative reinforcement. They are both the same in that they still reinforce the behaviour.

An example of a negative reinforcement is the absence of praise that was once present. The praise is the stimulus which is now removed. In response the person may start to increase their cigarette smoking, which previously they had reduced and received praise. The withdrawal of the praise (the stimuli) has actually negatively reinforced the continuation of the behaviour.

If a stimulus is removed from a situation which causes the behaviour to stop, then the behaviour has been extinguished. Recognise, however, that removing a stimulus can cause an increase in the unwanted behaviour.

For example, a mother stops praising the older child for playing with his younger sister (stimulus removed) and so he stops playing with her. That is extinction, but not the extinction outcome sought.

Sometimes when the stimulus (which has being reinforcing the behaviour) is removed, initially the behaviour will increase (because of negative reinforcement), but actually when the stimulus remains absent for a period of time, it eventually results in extinction of the behaviour. In other words, it takes time for the right outcome to be achieved, as there is adaptation to the removal of the stimulus.

What we do know is that if removing a stimulus from an existing behaviour, so as to extinguish that behaviour, is accompanied by adding a stimulus to a more desired behaviour (with the intention of positively reinforcing it), then extinction of the less desirable behaviour is likely to happen faster.

In other words, focus on a new behaviour which is more desirable, alongside an existing behaviour, may eventually cause the less desirable behaviour to extinguish. The more desirable behaviour can happen faster.

If for example, the older child's mother gave him attention by playing with him when he was being good, as well as ignoring him when he pushed his sister over, the less desirable behaviour would probably be extinguished quicker.

In CBT, wherever possible, the focus is actually to ignore the old behaviour. By ignoring it, you are removing all stimuli that kept the behaviour going, with the intention of extinguishing that old behaviour. At the same time/simultaneously – a new focus of thought, feeling, belief and behaviour in another direction, will positively reinforce a new behaviour. The old and the new will have difficulties continuing side by side. One must get less as the other gets more.

An important principle of learning is that in order to achieve behavioural change, the desired behaviour needs to be broken down into small manageable steps. It is achievement of success at each small manageable step which acts as a positive reinforcer to go on and continue to the next step. Therefore the new thoughts and behaviours have to be designed in a way that they are undertaken in small manageable steps. Frequently, failure is because the step undertaken to change a behaviour was too large.

An important concept of CBT is that the learning that comes out of the process has beneficial effects in other aspects of life. The skills can be used repeatedly.

4. Belief theories in CBT

The underlining theory behind CBT suggests that we have three levels of cognitions. They are core beliefs, intermediate beliefs and automatic thoughts.

Core beliefs: this is the most fundamental level of belief. Global, very rigid and over generalised. For example, *I am a failure. No-one likes me. Everything goes wrong when I touch it.*

The person may not always be consciously aware that they have them, but in fact they hold absolute truths, even though sometimes said in jest.

Intermediate beliefs: These are our sets of attitudes, rules and assumptions which come out of the influences of the core beliefs above. For example; if I come second, it shows I am a failure. If I win anything, there must be something wrong with the prize. Again the person is not always consciously aware of these beliefs.

Automatic thoughts: they are generated in given situations and stem out of the core belief and intermediate beliefs. This is as conscious as the awareness will get. For example, I must not do this. It is wrong.

Let us examine each of these in more detail. Past experiences have an effect on how we think and function. Bad experiences may have been endured and got over, but frequently they have left unpleasant memories and leave a mark not just in the present but also affect the future.

There are some tools enabling us to examine the effects of past experiences and how they might have led to us developing core beliefs that may be causing current emotional difficulties and behaviours. One to one therapy is really beneficial here.

CBT does not only focus intensively on childhood relationships and experiences, but also investigates how those past experiences may be affecting the present life.

The past can influence the present in a very significant way. Growing up with parents who fought a lot may have taught us to be very quiet and keep out of the way at those times so that any anger is not directed at us.

We may have had critical parents who made high academic demands, frequently interpreted as love and approval only when high achievements were attained. Not being able to predict the mood of a parent, who at times could be very violent when in a bad mood and at other times very loving and funny, may have left a legacy. Unfaithful partners causing frequent relationship break-ups, may cause insecurity and high levels of suspicion in current relationships.

Loss of a business, loss of a partner, death of a child, depression, teenage pregnancy all can paint a picture of being dogged with bad luck. In all of these situations, we can develop negative core beliefs and have a profound effect on our mental health. That contributes to the way that we think about ourselves, other people and the world.

Core beliefs are enduring ideas or core

philosophies, which we hold very strongly and very deeply. They are not always negative. Good experiences generally lead to healthy ideas about self, other people and the world. It is the negative core beliefs that we must concentrate on.

Core beliefs tend to be global and absolute and held to 100% under all conditions. They are often formed from childhood experiences and so never fully evaluated. They helped the child to make sense of the adult world and experiences. We may, however, continue to act, think and feel that way in adulthood. They are very central to our belief system.

Those core beliefs give rise to rules, demands, and assumptions and in turn produce automatic thoughts. Those automatic thoughts just pop into our head when we are confronted with a situation. Situations may arise from predisposing factors, precipitants and therefore we act them out so as to maintain them.

The core beliefs are so strong that they are used as lens or filters through which we interpret all the information we receive from other people and the world around us. Identifying your core beliefs can help you to understand why you keep having the same problems.

If core beliefs are held deeply we may not think of them or actually hear them in our own head as the clear statements that they are. It is probably more likely that we are more in tune with the negative automatic thoughts that arise out of the core beliefs.

More likely your core belief is leading you to take a prejudiced view of all your experiences. It is only when you put your finger on your core beliefs and identify those that are negative and unhealthy that you are in a position to develop healthier alternative beliefs.

The new core beliefs do not have to be extreme opposites. For example it may be changing "I'm bad" to "there are good things about me" or "I'm a failure" to "I succeed at some things".

Turning unhealthy and absolute core beliefs into alternatives is not about positive thinking, but it is about loosening our rigidity of thoughts and feelings and generating less absolute and more accurate, more realistic opinions about us, other people and the world around us. Time will be needed to move those new beliefs from our head to our heart.

Look at examples of aspects in our life which are rigid and only when you know about them, can you do something about them. What you can't see, you have little hope of affecting. What you can see, you have opportunity to affect. You now have choice!

Look again at your top 10 core emotional needs. When you know what those needs are then you can begin to understand some of the drivers that make you think, believe and act in the way that you do towards other people (at home, in the work place, socially and various situations).

Look also at the values which you hold. The exercise on values will have demonstrated how dear values are to us and the rigidity with which we hold to them, such that they are not easily changed or given up.

These exercises are not about changing our core beliefs or values or even giving them up. They are about recognition of things that go on in our lives and affect us, many of which we have no conscious knowledge. We are moving some things from the unconscious to the conscious. When we understand this much better, then we can start to examine what are our core beliefs and better understand how they can be working away in the unconscious. It is the negative core beliefs that we will seek to replace with new core beliefs over time.

5. Cognitive strategies

There may be set-backs in your endeavour to change. It is important to identify the nature of the set-back and perhaps a block that may have been reached.

Sometimes simple reassurance may unblock set-backs. It is important to continue attempts at change. If that strategy is not successful, then **cognitive restructuring** may be necessary.

First there is a need to identify the nature of the block; what is the feeling behind what has happened? What is the thought that generates the particular reaction causing the block? It is the beliefs behind the thought that needs to be identified. Only then are we in a position to examine and challenge the belief. The belief is challenged and examined by exploring the evidence for it.

If there is not sufficient evidence to support the belief, then the belief needs to be challenged. Perhaps an element of education by gaining information will help to challenge a belief. The belief may, after all, be based on false assumptions.

Understanding the factors which predispose towards the problem, the factors that are precipitating and also maintaining factors is necessary for setting appropriate tasks to achieve change. Also, understanding these factors is very useful in helping to unravel the core beliefs, which core beliefs sometimes block progress.

CBT to aid Change

The tools below are ones which are more effective when working with a therapist. They are mentioned below for information.

"....... no therapy is any more successful than the changes strategies that determined, persistent and hard working individuals develop for themselves." Prochaska, Norcross & DiClemente.

Behavioural modification

The aim of cognitive behaviour modification is to modify the following:

a) Thoughts and thinking styles
b) Self-talk and internal dialogues
c) Imagery associated with particular behaviours and settings
d) Maladaptive emotional reactions – to the extent that these are

cued and maintained by thought patterns and thinking styles.
Particular techniques include:

a) Use of imagery
b) Self inoculation training and self instruction
c) Cognitive restructuring
d) Relaxation therapy
e) Techniques for reducing anxiety and avoidance
f) Slow exposure and systematic desensitisation
g) Positive countering – conditioning
h) Rapid exposure techniques

In the formative learning years (which starts from a very young age and continues throughout life) an individual is exposed to stimulus and with that stimulus are associations. Those associations produce neutral, negative or positive feelings. It is the negative feelings which they produce and are associated with, which act as a stimuli for negative behaviours. As the dog associated food with the ringing of a bell, so we have learnt to associate certain behaviours.

Chapter 6

Ready now!

Changing your mind to change your life for better (2)

"Action springs not from thought, but from a readiness for responsibility" — *Dietrich Bonhoeffer*

Motivations to Change

Change interventions are sometimes necessary in life to address lifestyle modifications, aimed at preventing further issues or addictions. Motivation often focuses on the reasons for a person's failure. Understanding a person's readiness to make change, appreciating the barriers to change and helping individuals anticipate relapse, can better improve outcomes and reduce frustrations.

Promised improved outcomes do not guarantee long term motivation to change. Here are some theoretical assumptions about behaviour modification:

a) By far the greater portion of the behavioural repertoire which individuals already have has to do with learning.

b) Genetic and other physiological factors influence behaviour.

c) There are processes which cause us to acquire and maintain certain behaviours. These are classical (or respondent conditioning) and operand (or instrumental conditioning).

d) Behaviours judged to be abnormal are actually learned in exactly the same way as good behaviour is learned but we can, however, be predisposed to certain types of behaviours.

e) Properly applied, the technique from behaviour modification can have a direct and tangible effect on problematic behaviour.

Lessons from smoking and alcohol abuse

One size does not fit all. There are different interventions. Behavioural change has come to be understood as a process of identifiable stages of change. Those stages can be enhanced by taking specific action. Understanding the process provides additional tools.

For most people change in behaviour occurs gradually. A person moves from being uninterested, unaware or unwilling to make a change (pre contemplation), through considering change (contemplation), to deciding and preparing to make a change.

Genuine determined action is then taken. Over time, attempts to maintain the new behaviour occur. Relapses are almost inevitable and relapse actually becomes part of the process of working towards life-long change.

Before looking at those stages of change in more detail, let us look at the concept of motivational interviewing.

Motivational interviewing

The concept of motivational interviewing evolves from experience with the treatment of alcoholics. Motivational interviewing *is a directive client-centred counselling style for eliciting behaviour change by helping clients to explore and resolve ambivalence.*

The examination and resolution of ambivalence is the central purpose and goal being pursued by the Counsellor. The methods and techniques are characterised by the following:

1) Motivation to change comes from the client only.

2) Coercion, persuasion, constructive confrontation and use of external contingencies (for example the threat of loss of job or family) might sometimes work, but they are not within the spirit of motivational interviewing. Motivational interviewing is aimed at identifying and mobilising a person's own values and goals in order to stimulate an attitude towards behavioural change.

3) It is the person's task (not anyone else's) to articulate and resolve their own ambivalence. Ambivalence takes the form of a conflict between two courses of action. (For example, whether to indulge or to restrain). Each will have their perceived benefits and costs. (For example, if I stop smoking, I will feel better about myself, but I may also put on weight, which will make me feel unhappy and unattractive). The Counsellor's task is to give expression to both sides of the ambivalence and guide the person towards their own acceptable solution that might get them to a place where they decide on change.

4) Direct persuasion is not an effective method for resolving ambivalence. It is tempting in seeking to be helpful to endeavour to persuade people. What is clear, is that evidence shows that as a tactic, such endeavours generally increase the resistance to change and diminishes the probability of starting change. Also, it will affect the ability to maintain any perceived changes until the client is ready for change.

5) Counselling may be needed and the counselling style is generally a quiet and eliciting one: direct persuasion, aggressive confrontation, preaching, debating, arguing, justifying are all opposite to motivational interviewing technique. Pushing clients to make changes for which they are not ready can be counter productive.

6) The therapeutic relationship (which results from counselling) is more of a partnership or companionship, than the Counsellor taking an expert stance. The Counsellor respects the person's own autonomy and freedom of choice (as well as the consequences) for their own behaviour. Direct persuasion

and advice giving aimed at effecting change, is not motivational interviewing.

We may be wanting to change drinking habits, alcoholism, eating habits (excessive eating or addiction to a particular food), smoking, poor marital or other relational issues, other issues may include poor communication, parenting, problem with self esteem, failure to apply biblical standards (such as in the arena of sex, anger, temper, greed, hording, lack of consistent giving, gossiping, quick temper) inability to retain others confidences, inability to maintain relationships, addiction to drugs, sex, masturbation, pornography, shopping, food stuff. All are amenable to change.

Individuals move from being unaware or unwilling to consider the possibility of change, to becoming determined, prepared to make the change and actually actioning, sustaining and maintaining the change over time.

Self help courses are available, but otherwise the skilful help of a Counsellor/Therapist is significantly beneficial. Certainly, we will all need another person to help us, but one that is knowledgeable, since otherwise they can become a block or hindrance (particularly those that are close to us such as a partner). Relapse has to be handled well and with care to avoid long periods before getting back into the process of change.

Motives and motivation are needed in order to move from one stage of change to the next. It is not simply about moving through all the stages towards action. Resistances, ambivalence and commitment must be understood at each stage.

We therefore need to examine the stages of change.

We owe it to our children and the generation which will follow us, to be the best that we can be. That may involve us having to change, so that others benefit and not inherit our legacy, which may get passed on from generation to generation.

If a child lives with criticism

He learns to condemn.

If a child lives with hostility

He learns to fight.

If a child lives with ridicule

He learns to be shy.

If a child lives with shame

He learns to feel guilty.

If a child lives with tolerance

He learns to be patient.

If a child lives with encouragement

He learns confidence.

If a child lives with praise

He learns to appreciate.

If a child lives with fairness

He learns justice.

If a child lives with security

He learns to have faith.

If a child lives with approval

He learns to like himself.

If a child lives with acceptance and friendship

He learns to find love in the world.

The child soon becomes the man......

- Dorothy Law Nolte

The child soon becomes the woman/the man.

Chapter 7

Stages of Change

Before an individual can even begin the process of change they must know at what stage they are. Only when they know the stage they are at can they ensure the correct work is undertaken at that stage to move them to the next stage. This is of paramount importance.

Failure to know what stage the individual is at, is the reason that many fail. The right skills must be used at the right stage.

Pre contemplation

Individuals at this stage are not even thinking about changing the problem behaviour. They may not even see the behaviour as a problem or believe that it is problematic, even if others think it is a problem. They may be addicted to the behaviour and there may be resistance or a block towards change or they may be in denial.

The four R's of Reluctance, Rebellion, Resignation and Rationalisation apply.

The reluctant pre contemplator may lack knowledge or inertia to do what they want to do to even consider change. Information about the problem or its impact has not become fully considered. They are reluctant to change.

The rebellious pre contemplator have a vested interest in maintaining the problem. They are resistant to being told what to do. Preaching at them and telling them to change may hit a rebellious wall. The rebellion may be a resistance arising from childhood insecurities and fears.

The rebellious pre contemplator may appear hostile and quite resistant to change and be very set in their ways. It can be quite easy to spot the rebels. They argue with even the questions. They make it clear that they will participate and even attend, as long as they are not going to be forced to try to change.

Interestingly enough, such individuals use a lot of energy maintaining the problem by resisting any attempts at being told what to do. If that energy can be utilised in another way, they actually have a lot of energy that can be put into the process of effecting change. They become good candidates, if the rebellion can be overcome.

The resigned pre contemplators are very much the opposite. They lack even energy. They have given up on the possibility of change. They are overwhelmed by the problem. They can count how many attempts they have made in the past to overcome and have failed. They feel hopelessly addicted and that the problem is somewhat out of control. They know they have a habit and a tendency and that the habit is actually in control and they are out of control. They see ways to avoid the problem occurring to other people, but have lost heart that change will ever happen for them. They think it is too late.

The motivational interviewing skills that can be used at this stage are to instil hope by exploring the barrier to change.

The rationalising pre contemplator has all the answers (very different to the resigned pre contemplator who has none). Rationalising pre contemplators are not considering change because they have weighed up all the risks and odds or have plenty of reasons why the problem is not really such a big problem for them.

What happens is that they have a conversation within themselves and you can frequently hear it being voiced in discussions with others including in the therapy room. Discussions feel like a debate for scoring points. It may feel like rebellion or even resistance, but the difference is in their thinking. They may think they are not at much risk of adverse consequences, because things are not so bad. The very fact of a discussion, debate or argument is what feeds their rationalising.

There is a difference between a risk and rationalising. Some people may genuinely know what the risks are and accept those risks and are not rationalising. They may be seen as unreasonable, but they have assessed the risks. They have exercised their freedom to choose the particular behaviour. They can still be helped towards contemplating change, but the limit of any motivational strategies must be acknowledged.

Contemplation

There is a willingness to consider the problem and the possibility of change offers hope. However, ambivalence is present. Change is wanted, but often something is awaited (an extra push, a piece of information or something) – just one final piece of information that will compel the move to change.

The ambivalence (a conflict between two opposing choices) is that the behaviour actually served a purpose. There will be a sense of loss if it changes or goes, despite the perceived benefits. There is knowledge of the benefits of change and the need for change and the advantages of change, but there are disadvantages.

The hope is that final piece of information will help to tip the scales and the balance and make the decision for us. The fact is, however, that it is the individual who needs to make the decision and not the information that is awaited and therefore we can remain in this contemplation stage for a very, very long, unproductive wait.

When one piece of information comes, it may shift to needing something else and moving towards change becomes elusive. Very importantly, contemplation of change is not commitment to change. This must be understood. Do not be misled by the distinction.

Consideration has to be given to the costs of changing. Not considering the costs may later on cause relapse. Ambivalence is the main enemy to commitment to change and a prime reason for remaining stuck at the contemplation stage.

Determination

This stage is marked by a definite decision to take steps to overcome the problem behaviour. It is a determination to commence the process to effect change and the intention to commence that programme in the near future. There is an appearance of being ready for and commitment to action. This stage represents a preparation and not just a determination.

The decision making process – to commence change – is a continuous process and continues throughout this stage. Strong commitment alone does not guarantee commencing change or achieving change. Enthusiasm will not make up for poor attempts. Willpower alone will often not be sufficient to stay the course and then to maintain the change. Willpower can become a drain on energy.

Action

You have made the plan and have a strategy in place, ready to implement. It is easy to cancel further appointments because you feel you are going great, when in fact ongoing support is vital. A part of the strategy in the action stage may include recognising triggers; triggers for addictive behaviour to predict outcomes before they occur; to intervene to avoid relapse.

Life style enhancement needs to be considered. Giving up a particular addictive behaviour may result in more free time. How to spend that free time needs to be thought about and planned. Perhaps attending group meetings become necessary (like AA). That might add colour to life and even become a social outlet. It is important to revitalise other interests to replace the addictive behaviour.

The next stages are **maintenance**, **relapse** and **recycling**.

The action stage might take between 3 – 6 months to complete. This is because any addictive behaviour requires a new pattern of behaviour to be built in before effective change can be maintained. It takes a while to establish a new pattern of behaviour. The real test is the extent to which it is long term, sustained change over several years. This last stage is therefore called "maintenance".

The threat of relapse or return to the old pattern becomes less frequent and less intense because the new behaviour is maintained. Relapse is always possible in the action stage or in the maintenance stage. It can occur for different reasons.

There may be a strong, unexpected urge or temptation which the individual fails to cope with successfully. Sometimes the guard may be relaxed or testing oneself too far can cause the relapse. Sometimes the cost involved in maintaining the change is not well calculated. Often the relapse is a gradual process.

Within the maintenance stage new practice needs to become automatic. Just like learning an instrument requires practice, so it is that repeated implementation of a new behaviour will make the past addictive behaviour become less and less and the new behaviour takes centre stage.

A slip-up or relapse should not mean throwing in the towel. It is important to assess what has been achieved to date and build on that.

For example, an alcoholic may feel they have relapsed because they had a glass of champagne at a wedding reception. They may beat themself up afterwards and feel like giving up totally.

If they recognise that they did slip-up by having one glass of champagne, they need to recognise that they did not have a second glass! That is a true achievement and actually it could be classed as a successful relapse.

Beating oneself up will de-motivate and actually cause the old behaviour to flood back in – because there was much comfort (albeit temporary comfort) gained from the old behaviour.

Is it possible that in fact you do not have more problems than most other people, you just think abut them more often? (One problem is though, enough to get our attention and want to eradicate it). Recognise, however, that it is what you think about which dictates how you feel.

Try this exercise

Try to get angry without first having angry thoughts – without having a reason and focus for your anger. I know that is very artificial, but try!

Try getting angry without first having a sad thought.

Finding it difficult or can you do it?

You see – in order to experience a feeling, you must first have the thoughts and it is the thoughts which produce the feelings. If you therefore change your thinking (your mind), then you can change how you feel and thus change the direction in which your day goes and eventually you will change your life. (That piece of knowledge alone is worth the price of this book)!

Chapter 8

Conflicts

"Dear Sir: Regarding your article 'What's Wrong with the World?' I am. Yours truly," —
<u>G.K. Chesterton</u>

The vast majority of words that we think about conflict are negative ones. Conflict should not always be viewed as being negative. Let us define conflict as "a difference in opinion or purposes that frustrates someone's hopes or desires". Many conflicts are caused or aggravated by wrong attitudes or actions.

I may look at my wife with a twinkle in my eyes as she is getting dressed to go to work. Her thoughts may well be "No way, I will be late for work!". At that moment in time there is a "difference in opinion" - the potential for a minor conflict! Do I need help to resolve that conflict, if it develops? Probably not. Why? As long as one of us changes our mind, I guess the issue will dissipate. I can change what I can affect – me and my mind. That should be my focus. I could also try to change that which I do not have the ability to control – the other person; and have much less chance of doing so.

This story is told of an old Rabbi:

> *"When I was young, I set out to change the world. When I grew a little older, I perceived that this*

was too ambitious, so I set out to change my State. This too, I realised as I grew older, was too ambitious, so I set out to change my Town. When I realised I could not even do this, I tried to change my family. Now, as an old man, I know that I should have started by changing myself. If I had started with myself, then I would have succeeded in changing my family, the Town or even the State and who knows, maybe even the world".

Our tendency is to try to get the other person to change so as to meet our want. That may trigger a reaction in the other person who may want to maintain the status quo. Men frequently practice "flight" from a situation and that can take the form of the silent treatment. This exasperates the situation and taps into the woman's fear of feeling disconnected. Storge and Phileo love (two of the greek words for love which we look at later) are disrupted. She feeds off his behaviour and he in turn starts to feed off hers. Both of them are feeling disconnected from each other – having lost the Phileo best friend. Neither is getting their need met (like we see in the stubborn mule diagram).

We need to take personal responsibility for our actions and reactions. We do have control, but we cannot permanently control other people. We cannot control another person's reaction, but we can control our reaction.

We need to change the pattern. Yet it is important to know that some do not want to change and do not want to give up the pattern because actually, it acts as a regulator in the relationship. It actually regulates the extent of closeness in relationships. Where rejection is a trait from childhood experience - which many do not recognise as a trait within them – regulating the closeness of the relationship is a must. Arguing and making up becomes a common and necessary feature.

Therefore some do not actually want to remain too close. When they feel too close they unconsciously throw a hand grenade into the relationship to destroy it for a while. Remember, it is done unconsciously and creates the arguments which disrupt harmony and closeness until making up is desired by them.

There are four main causes of Conflict. **Misunderstandings**, resulting from poor communication; **differences in values**, goals, priorities, expectations, interests or opinions; **competition** over limited resources, such as time or money and finally, **Wrong doing**.

Conflict is not necessarily bad. Some differences are natural and beneficial. We are unique individuals and therefore we will have different opinions, convictions, desires, perspectives and priorities. That is a part of our diversity and personal preferences. Disagreements can stimulate productive dialogue, encourage creativity, promote helpful exchange and generally make life more interesting. Unity does not demand uniformity. We should not be seeking to avoid conflict, but rejoice in diversity.

It is very hard to remain in conflict with someone you are touching and embracing. The block is letting go of pride and actually making the first move to touch the other person. You should try it!

Instead we do go to sleep on our anger. The unresolved conflict will delay sleep. We play the game. We pretend we are sleeping and it is then a battle of who will give in first. The rules are well practiced. Don't move at all so the other thinks you are sleeping and not concerned that you have fallen out with each other! Even the quilt falling off us in the night and feeling a little cold, is not enough to cause movement because we are playing the game of pretend sleep. Breathing is even exaggerated in case the other should not realise that we are truly sleeping! You want to itch, but just can't for fear of giving yourself away. The 2.30am conflict resolution chat can begin if the other person will begin first. Sound familiar? You must have played that game as well!

Hurt turns to want; want turns to fear; fear causes us to react; as we react it hurts; as you hurt you want; as you want, you are fearful of something and as you become fearful of something you react and so the cycle of feeding off each other continues and the relationship is in crisis and moves from lukewarm to a boiling point. Something will tip it over the edge. It is so much better to be in control of change rather than change being done to you – often in a way you had not really wanted.

When our core emotional needs or values are not being met, we either fight or flight – in order to regain connectedness or get back control. We will do anything to avoid the feeling of "want". Our reaction is to try to get the other person to change so as to meet our want; that triggers the core fear in the other person who in turn reacts to get their wants met.

All our deepest fears stem from our desire for connection (to be secure) and significance. Our deepest fears are therefore to lose connection and lack significance.

There are 7 **A's of an effective confession**. They are:

1. **Address** everyone involved: admit to your role which contributed to the conflict - to every person who has been directly affected.

2. **Avoid** "if", "but" and "maybe": do not use words that shift the blame to others or appear to minimise or excuse

your guilt.

3. **Admit** specifically: identify the specific behaviour which you need to change.

4. **Acknowledge** the hurt: show that you are trying to understand the way someone must have felt by your behaviour.

5. **Accept** the consequence: the consequence may have been severe and restitution may be necessary.

6. **Alter** your behaviour: explain to the person you offended how you plan to alter your behaviour in the future. Maybe the change/CBT work outlined above is for you!

7. **Ask** for forgiveness (and allow the other person time).

Do not use the process as a ritual. It will show itself up as having been meaningless.

Forgiveness. Me!

"If you board the wrong train, it is no use running along the corridor in the other direction" — <u>*Dietrich Bonhoeffer*</u>

Maybe a specific form of apology is called for. It may need to take the form of a request for forgiveness. A request for forgiveness seems to be a dying art. We have developed a mentality of blame culture and it must always be someone else's fault – not ours.

Think carefully about what you do when you ask for forgiveness. It can heal a lot of wounds, but it can be costly! Here is what an effective request for forgiveness looks like. These are the 4 hallmarks that you are promising:

- I will not dwell on the incident.

- I will not bring the incident up and use it against you.

- I will not talk to others about the incident.

- I will not allow the incident to stand between us or hinder our personal relationship.

That's a mighty tall order! The reality is that your own unforgiveness of someone who you feel has wronged you will eat away at you and build a wall of opposition so that it becomes harder and harder to be reconciled. Forgiveness is not about forgetting or excusing. The memories do not just leave us. It is an active process whereby you chose not to dwell on the incident and in time the details of it will fade. You chose not to churn it around in your mind when it seeks pride of place in your thoughts. Time will be the healer. You don't just forget!

The **P   A   U   S   E** principle for negotiating

with someone assists us to prepare beforehand. Used alongside the communication skills we look at below, these principles represent practical steps we should take to prepare:

- **Prepare** – get the facts; identify issues and interests, consider options; anticipate reactions; consider alternatives; select appropriate time and place to talk; plan opening remarks; and seek input from another.

- **Affirm** relationships – affirm your respect for the person (despite the way you are feeling). Express your appreciation for their willingness to listen to you.

- **Understand** Interest – it is important to know the difference between an issue, position and an interest :

    An Issue – is an identifiable and concrete question that must be addressed in order to reach an agreement (ie the issue is what the conflict is about).

    A Position – is where a party stands on an issue. What is their stance and perspective?

    An Interest – is what motivates people. It is a concern, desire, need or something a person values. (ie what is their true motive for wanting a particular outcome).

Interest provide the basis for our positions and when we know the interest, we are better able to find a solution.

We need to find out what is the real issue. Counsellors have a way of doing that. We use circular questioning by asking (for example) "so what...", "why is that a problem..." or "so what if..."

All of these questions are aimed at getting to the heart/core of the problem. At the core of the problem is a particular fear. It might be fear of failure, not being loved, not being in a family or being lonely. Something is driving and feeding the real problem, but we put forward particular facades. The problem voiced is often not the real problem.

- **Search** - for creative solutions. Think creatively to find a mutually satisfying solution.

- **Evaluation** options objectively and reasonably. Make sure it is the best possible solution for you both. This is very difficult to do when you are in conflict. That is why a separation period at the time of conflict is rarely a wise option. During that separation, it is challenging indeed to think many good things about the other person. We focus more on the wrong done to us and the snowball becomes an avalanche!

Be a peacemaker in your relationship. You do not need to think that you will then be viewed as weak and vulnerable to being walked all over. It is a good quality. Strive after it!

Discord in the relationship is the most common reason for sexual dysfunction.

Chapter 9

LOVE: Rebuilding, Refreshing, Resurrecting, Rekindling

Falling in love may be involuntary – some say! What is certain is that remaining in love is a choice. We can choose to fall out of love. Love does not just go. It takes time. Coasting in the relationship means a downward incline! The downward spiral is not always immediately visible. We can justify the reasons for the disharmony only for so long before the extent of the rift is visible for all to see.

I do wonder about the concept of "Love at first sight". Is it rather "attraction at first sight?" Love takes time to develop. You will see that more clearly as we look at the five loves.

Childhood experiences, whether good, bad or indifference do have a profound effect upon our beliefs about our self and our expectations of others. Most of us fail to appreciate that or take it into account when we run into difficulties in later life. It is amplified in the intimacy of the relationship.

Some conflicts in relationship can be seen as an attempt by individuals to put right experiences of the past. Relationship is the place of our healing. Don't leave your place of healing too soon!

Love so often fail us - it would seem. There may be a misconception of love. Could it be that many do not have a clear understanding of what love truly is? Maybe we do not actually know how to love. Even though the vows are said or the commitment given, in many cases there has not been a heart and mind unconditional decision and resolve to commitment to love for a life time. It is quietly and secretly conditional upon you continuing to...!

Many of our behaviour and responses to our partner are influenced by our own concept and misconception about love. We may have faulty conclusions based on experience. Personal experience sometimes provides flawed views or misinformation so that we reach faulty conclusions.

It is on the foundation of those flawed views that so often we enter into the union and seek to build a lasting and loving relationship. As in the Pinch & Crunch diagram (Chapter3), we carry within us and into the relationship, good and not so good stuff. The stuff mostly came from our family upbringing experiences - from the most formative people in our early growing up years. The stuff may have served us satisfactorily for a season until now – this relationship! Then it doesn't serve us well anymore!

The problem is that we ignore or pay insufficient attention to such things as our own culture, age, sexuality, race, morals, ethics and the various diversities which make us unique. The way in which those things have shaped us so often underpin our experiences.

Television, radio, school, college, university, books, magazines and various media, all shape and contribute to formulating our beliefs. We now have "stuff" in our mindsets which we take into the relationship and the Pinch and Crunch experiences now play themselves out, because the other person also has come with their diversity, flaws, misconception of love and relationships. It is inevitable that our view of love will shape our behaviour towards our partner. What if we have a flawed view about what love really is?

We can choose to love and therefore choose not to love. Choose to love. It is a choice. Then follow through with action. This book will help you with action and practical application. Love is not simply doing what comes naturally. It is costly. It is a valuable gift. It is sacrificial. We live in an age and time when "sacrifice" has strong connotations of being an underdog or servitude! It need not be so!

We can learn a new way of loving. We can learn to love again. Learning to love again is not very different from the processes involved in learning and perfecting something to which we put our hands, such as learning a trade, a new hobby, musical instrument or anything else that requires discipline! We have to learn the technique, apply it and practice it. That sounds rather mechanical! It is, however, a fundamental truth which has to be realised, accepted and acted upon – practice, practice and more practice!

In order to master the art of loving and obtain the rewards, we have to learn the principles of building love into our relationship and practising them on a daily basis.

Chapter 10

Love me in five ways (1)

Most of us operate out of emotional love. Our love is conditional. If we are to learn a better way then change will be demanded. If this teaching gets into our hearts, we cannot remain the same. Change can be uncomfortable. It may mean a turnaround is required; a turn from a way of being; a turn from a way of behaving and a way of operating. Not everyone will accept this teaching. Not everyone will want to accept it.

Loving self comes first. If you do not love yourself it is not possible to love someone with the high level of love you think you have for them. I know you may want to challenge me about this! It is deception to think that we do love our partner, whilst not really able to say that we love our self. We are being untrue but cannot see that the truth is not in us. You are betraying both of you. Learn to love yourself first. This then is yet another place to put this book down and ponder the issue of love of self. You can only love as much as you understand love. Individual counselling may be necessary to help you on the journey.

Learn to love and then learn the art of practising love. Learn it well and then spend a lifetime in discipline, maintaining and perfecting it as your love affair. Men may not need to hear the words "I love you" as often as women, but for sure they need to know they are valued and respected and they receive them from demonstrable acts and voice of appreciation. Men, do not refrain from using those words "I Love you" for long, even when there is plenty of flower giving, taking out and sex! Be warned.

We know that the English word *love* is much over used. We use it as much for loving a meal as we do for loving our partner, the pet or ice cream. Using one word in that manner is a recipe for misunderstanding and certainly lacks precision in what we are trying to express.

We can compare that to the way the word love is broken down and used in the Greek language. Historically the Greek language used at least five words precisely and quite distinctly to describe the various facets of love.

By looking at each of those different word descriptions we can build up the identifying features of all the components that the word *love* should contain and demonstrate in all healthy, progressive and fulfilling relationships. Those five words for love are **Epithumia, Eros, Phileo, Storge** and **Agape**.

Every couple's love life should have all five facets of these aspects of love. Each builds on the other. Each has its own special and significant place. Each is distinct, but inter-related and overlaps. Each reinforces the other. Don't forget that! Let's look at the first of those five loves.

EPITHUMIA: (The sexual love)

Epithumia is a strong desire - of any kind. As a strong desire it can be sometimes good and sometimes bad. It is a longing for something or someone. It is to set one's heart or desire upon. Therefore it can be viewed as having components of coveting and to lust after. We only come across the word lust as a negative expression. This is one instance when it can be used positively. It is a strong lustful and physical sexual desire in the context of a married man and woman, one toward the other. Therefore in relationship husband and wife should have a strong physical desire for each other that goes on to express itself in pleasurable sexual love making.

Even in the happiest of relationships couples can improve their sexual relationship through increased knowledge and understanding about sexual matters. Let's define how we are using the words "sexual intercourse". It is not limited to the contact of the genitals, but covers the whole preparation and progression towards sexual activity. Therefore sexual intercourse includes foreplay and foreplay commences even before getting home! Foreplay is the unexpected phone call received whilst at work; the text message of affection and the love note in the others pocket.

Whilst sexual intercourse is not the most important aspect of the relationship, it certainly is a thermometer for testing the temperature and pulse of the relationship. It is a definite indicator of the health of the relationship. If tension exists, the first aspects that will show up are the difficulties in the sex life.

Frequently what we will do is start kidding ourselves with excuses and seemingly good logical reasons when our sexual relationship is lacking. Even when the relationship is floundering we can still have mutual pleasure in our sex life. That should be the case, whilst at the same time the couple are working through the other missing facets of love; perhaps in counselling/therapy.

Sex therapy is well recognized as a specialised counselling field where treatment is available for dysfunctions and disorders in the sexual side of the relationship. I am well practiced in that field and work with clients by Skype quite effectively. Sexual addiction and compulsivity is a burgeoning field of

practice, particularly as our knowledge increases about the significant addictive qualities of internet pornography and cybersex use. I am a member of the association for the treatment of sexual addiction & compulsivity.

Human sexual development

The route to us achieving sexual maturity has been a complicated journey with many ports, tangents and departures. Even before birth, important stages were laying down some milestones for our future sexuality. Childhood sexual experiences can be associated with sexual difficulties in adulthood. Throughout childhood and early adolescence various strands of our development combine to produce the sexual adult. That sexual adult continues to develop sexually throughout life. There are a multitude of influences. Our sexual map was developing and that determined our sexual template of preferences, including fetishes!

All of us have learnt a sexual script. Our brain holds that sexual script. The script can be re-written if we know what it is. But most of us do not know it. A part of that sexual script has to do with what we were taught about sex or what we picked up.

Sigmund Freud enlightens us with some knowledge which has helped us in our understanding. He suggests to us that children show masturbatory behaviours until they learn about shame from adults and then it becomes a secret and private thing in which the child and their curiosity may continue to indulge. A study in1974 showed that infant boys begin to play with their genitals at about 6 to 7 months and girls at 10 to 11 months. Boys continue until obvious masturbation is established at 15 to 16 months.

Girls showed more intermittent genital play and more tendency to transfer to less direct methods of stimulation. By age 20, 92% of men had masturbated compared to one third of women. By age 40 some 62% of women had masturbated. Where men did masturbate, it was two to three times more frequent. Singleness masturbation before the couple relationship can continue to be a problem within the relationship. Having a sexual partner tends to increase (rather than decrease) the frequency of male masturbation.

We know that childhood sexual abuse is much more prevalent than had previously been thought. There are a large proportion of people that have suffered sexual abuse as a child and have learnt ways to "forget about it" or cope with it. The dilemma is that sometimes it seeps out. If we or our partner, do not know about that past, then it may be influencing our sexual behaviour. Maybe that script needs some help to be re-written.

By the way "Shame" is a very significant (and never to be under estimated) feature in sex addiction - which feeds it!

The sexual response cycle

There is a difference between male and female in the way their bodies behave and re-act to sexual stimulation leading to sexual intercourse. It is important to understand those differences.

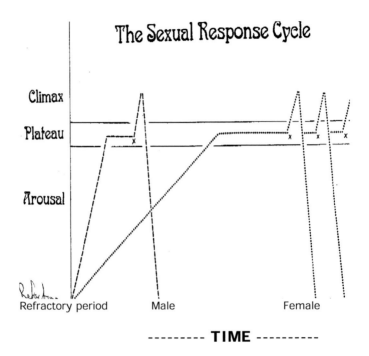

The sexual response cycle explains those differences. They are the changes that occur during sexual arousal as a response to sexual stimulation of any kind. It is plotted on a graph above.

A debt is owed to Masters and Johnson for their work on sexual responses in both men and women. Masters and Johnson acknowledge the contribution provided by the earlier work of Kinsey and others. Some time later Kaplan identified a first phase which applies to women – that of Desire and that

87

was added to the sexual response cycle.

The sexual response cycle starts with desire for the woman, leading to excitement, plateau, orgasm and resolution phases. The male will not always have desire and may start from the excitement phase. Desire is subjective and not measurable, unlike the other phases. It has qualities that represent the emotional states of hunger and wanting food. Others view it as sexual interest or libido. Studies show clearly that a poor relationship with a partner does predict low sexual desire. Where anxiety lives, desire will remain inhibited. Some women have responsive, rather than spontaneous desire. In other words they respond to stimuli such as touch.

The second phase of excitement represents mostly changes from increased flow of blood to the genital organs and other blood vessels causing engorgement and lubrication. As excitement intensifies the second phase or plateau of high sexual arousal or tension, results in a levelling off of arousal and immediately precedes the threshold level of arousal necessary to trigger orgasm. Continued stimulation results in the third stage of orgasm, where involuntary release of sexual tension occurs in pleasurable rhythmic pattern and then dissipation of sexual tension.

During the fourth stage of *resolution* the anatomical and physiological changes start to dissipate and return to their normal unaroused state, contributing to a feeling of relaxation and well-being. This is an important phase for completing the full sexual response cycle of sexual intercourse and is a time when a couple can share their feelings for each other through the experience of a unique sense of closeness, promoted by a sense of relaxation and relaxed muscle tone.

It is a time of bonding and rebonding between the couple with something Spiritual having just taken place. It is the height of the oneness. Don't break the bond of closeness too quickly by rushing to the bathroom to clean up. Sex is messy!

The duration of the phases differ between men and women. Typically, the duration of the excitement phase is longer for women and is a very important phase for ensuring sufficient vaginal lubrication before attempts by the penis to enter the vagina without causing pain. There is much more that could be said about each phase.

Another notable difference between males and females is a *refractory period* for males. That means after one ejaculation there is a period when they are unable to experience another ejaculation or orgasm. The length of that period depends very much upon factors which include age, desire and the effects of alcohol or medication. Women have the potential to have one orgasm after another. They are multi-orgasmic. Some women have not and do not achieve an orgasm. Sex therapy has the very real potential to change that if the couple desire change.

Sex can be used to punish, frustrate, reject or pay back. It can be turned off deliberately, purposefully and by choice. The quiet treatment, criticism, suspicion, anger, hurt, silence, misunderstanding, fear, hostility or guilt having their tentacles in the relationship. These will be hindrances and play a part in shutting down certain stages in the sexual responses. Anxiety, self-consciousness, scoring and performance pressures are some other attitudes and behaviours which will affect phases in the sexual response cycle.

Sex therapists are assisted in their work by having a good understanding of pre-disposing, precipitants and maintaining factors which are psychological causes of sexual dysfunction. The dysfunctions include lack of orgasm by either party; pain for either during penetrative sex; male erectile difficulties; inability to allow the penis into the vagina; premature ejaculation or lack of desire or interest in sex.

Pre-disposing factors from early childhood experiences may arise from overt or covert messages about sex. They may arise because of a restrictive upbringing, perception about the quality of relationships between parents, inadequate sexual information and traumatic early sexual experiences (of which childhood sexual abuse is a key factor). Also early insecurity in own psychosexual role, such as lack of comfort with personal sexuality and
90

therefore an adverse view about sexual identity, masturbation, own body development, as well as other people's view of self – all can contribute to sexual disorders/dysfunctions.

Precipitants are events, circumstance and situations associated with and connected to the sexual problem. When certain circumstances are recognised as present they act as a precipitant to the problem actually occurring. Precipitants may be physical or psychological. They restrict the sexual response.

Precipitants include loss of interest by a woman following childbirth; discord in the general relationship (which may also then become a maintaining factor); cheating - such as an affair or other guilt and secrets; unreasonable expectations (where things such as inability to achieve multiple orgasms, not "coming" together and sexual myths are active). One partner may suffer random failure, of which stress, alcohol, medication and drugs are contributors. Reaction to organic factors (such as heart attack), ageing and issues around physiological changes from ageing, depression and anxiety, as well as other traumatic sexual experiences (such as rape and unwanted pregnancy) - are precipitant.

Maintaining factors are those things which are present and explain why the problem continues. It may be performance anxiety.

91

That will inhibit the natural sexual response cycle. Hand in hand with anxiety is anticipation of failure, which may lead to guilt. Loss of attraction between the partners, poor communication, discord in the general relationship, impaired or poor self image, inadequate sexual information, knowledge and sexual myths (which are also precipitants) - are also maintainers. Alongside are such things as insufficient foreplay, psychiatric disorders and alcoholism.

I single out the fear of intimacy for further mention because fear of prolonged intimacy may cause avoidance or limited contact between the couple in case it leads further than one of them wants. They desire affection and contact, especially when sex is not working well for them. Yet contact is avoided and limited so as to regulate the frequency of attempting to have sexual intercourse, which evoke such strong memories of failure. A lose/lose dilemma and a spiralling vicious circle is established.

The need for sex therapy is readily identifiable in all of the scenarios above. The benefits of sex therapy are available to the elderly who want an active sex life, as well as those who suffer from various disabilities and are so often are not well catered for in other fields.

Correct knowledge is a starting point. There may be misconceptions, misinformation, false teachings, wrong views - all of which may have to be challenged, discarded and right thinking replace them, based on correct information. Understand that you can turn off your interest in sex and can turn off (at least) the capacity for sex.

The healthy sexual life requires the development and maintaining a life time love affair. Even if you already have a good relationship, it can be better! You have a right to expect and anticipate increased sexual pleasure year after year. You have no right to expect diminished sexual pleasure. Diminished sexual pleasure need not come with older age and certainly need not stay. In middle age and senior years sensitive, uninhibited practiced love making can become exhilarating with a partner who responds and performs in a complementary way.

We have been left with a very bad image of sex and a legacy throughout history and particularly from the Victorian age. Some will witness to the fact that they knew little about sex and later realised how much their parents' disapproval and negative images have left a negative impression upon them. It may take years to let go of and give self permission to embrace and enjoy sex. Many picked up what they knew from magazines, library books or school kids talk. Sexual myths became entrenched and were believed and practiced for a long time. May be even now!

We must love our body as our own. We would not hurt our own body. Therefore unreasonable demands are of course not acceptable, since we would not do anything to hurt one's own body. Having unreasonable sexual demands is to try to hurt own body and the other person. What is unreasonable demand? That is something for the two of you to discuss and negotiate over, but always with an eye on the fact that we must not do harm to self or others – physically, emotionally, sexually or otherwise.

Sex without signs of love is sure to create resentment, not response. Prepare the ground for lovemaking long before the sexual act itself takes place. Use affectionate pats, text messages and other ways to endear you to your partner. Admiring glances across the crowded room makes the person feel and know they are special. These acts are foreplay. They commence before getting home!

Once you are together you should shut out the world. Ensure complete privacy, particularly from children. Use a lock if it will aid relaxation for one more than the other. Fear of being caught in the act is an inhibitor for many.

Don't take the sexual relationship so seriously. Don't aim for simultaneous orgasm on every occasion. Keep sex light-hearted and fun. It should be recreational; especially so, since it is suppose to be regular and for a lifetime! If it is hard work, then sooner or later it will diminish. Initially it probably will be an effort, but as you work at it, it should become recreational pleasure.

Women do not always need or desire an orgasm during sexual intercourse. Husbands find that hard to understand because we view it from our male bodily response and expectation. "Did the earth move for you?" is an intimidating question to ask the other person just after love making. What can they say – especially if the earth did not move! Men are guiltier of asking the question. Wait until a different occasion if it has to be asked - because it was not witnessed! Begin to learn about your wife's reactions during the sexual response phases and soon you will not need to ask!

Vicious cycles can be created within relationships and maintained for many years. The wife feels a failure because she cannot work up the right physical response leading to an orgasm. She tries harder. As she tries harder the more the natural reflex action required for an orgasm fades. She begins to sense her husband's disapproval or disappointment and the sex act becomes increasingly painful physically and emotionally.

She begins to avoid sex. If her husband persists, she feels used. Resentment sets in. A low self image may begin to appear and soon she begins to think that her husband only has ulterior motives when he is being nice to her. Our mouth betrays us with words that slip out and we did not even know that such levels of resentment had built up inside our hearts.

The husband's confidence may become shaken by the sense of failure at not being able to bring sexual release to his wife. As his wife begins to avoid sex, he may get the feeling that she is no longer interested in him. He begins to wonder if she even loves him. They are on a downward spiral. A vicious circle has set in. The stage is set for dysfunctions.

Remember, orgasms happen in the brain not the genitals and so the focus of our attention can be the very thing which disrupts and hinders orgasm.

Barriers build up from persistent discouragement. The sense of rejection, inadequacy and failure needs to be broken. The couple will need to turn away from concentration on sexual climax and the problems of sex and relearn how to enjoy each other without the pressures of sexual intercourse. Ban sexual intercourse for a period. Stick to it and use the same amount of time to explore each others bodies without sexual intercourse.

Only you stand between your situation and the solution.

Chapter 11

Love me in five ways (2)

EROS: (Romance)

The second of our five loves is Eros. The word has been corrupted by the English word "erotic". Eros is the driver for the romance in the relationship. Sometimes sensual, it is the idea, desire and feeling of wanting to be together and yearning to unite; to possess the other, such is the intensity of the feelings.

Eros is romantic, passionate and sentimental. It is so readily visible in the early days of the developing relationship. It is the driver which causes lovers to write love poetry, love notes and give pet names for each other – piggy wiggy! The impulse to miss the train or bus easily wins, even though it is pouring with rain because a small gift is spotted in a shop window which you desire to buy. The radiant smile of the receiver makes the detour so worthwhile.

The problem is that there are limitations with eros. It has elements of infatuation. It is based on what we are getting back from the other. It keeps working as long as there is reciprocation and we can see benefits; but it cannot keep up appearance on its own. It is changeable as the relationship changes. It needs help to keep the promise – that we will be together for a lifetime. The other four loves must complement it. It cannot last for a lifetime by itself, despite promises and genuine belief to that effect.

Most of us long to get back that indescribable sensation and feeling of "being in love". We experience it for a while at the beginning of the relationship, but over time it faded until we do not even remember the feeling. The best we get is resurgence for a short lived period, when the right movie hits the spot and a scene reminds us of what we use to have. We recognise what we have lost but quickly snap out of the day dream. We accept it is gone forever. Familiarity with each other took it away. Expectation of its return is unrealistic and illusory.

We came off of cloud nine long ago. We no longer feel energised or motivated to do those things which we would previously have done, such as going out to the sport centre and getting exercise so that our physical looks are more attractive to our partner; driving for many many miles for just a few hours to be with the one we love and then driving many hours back again - during the working week!

The feelings of falling out of love are amplified by the pressure that life brings. We know that relationships can change drastically for the worse when couples become parents. Not having planned the pregnancy; alienation from each other because roles were not negotiated and resentment set in when stereotypical role fulfilment was thrust upon each of them. Fathers losing their bride to a child and pregnancy resentment; stress of a third person in the relationship; no one to talk to about those feelings we should not be having or thinking when it is suppose to be a joyous occasion; no family nearby to help out – all take a toll.

Eros love provided that energy, that motivation, that confidence, that sensation of being in love. As the years have gone by it is lost. Well! You can bring it back into your relationship to enhance the excitement and build on it year by year. That is so, even if you are having very serious problems in your relationship.

When everything between the two of you seems to have gone wrong, the routine of relationship life is well set in. Life is being lived for an unknown next event. Maybe you are staying just until the kids have left school or home. But speak quietly, I have not even told myself that is what I am waiting for! Maybe the answer is to fall in love again.

Maybe you some time ago acknowledged a painful thought – that you do not feel as if you any longer love your partner. That has been a harsh bitter tablet to swallow and accept. Could it be that "feelings" are not telling you the truth? The answer is to fall in love again. If you have the will to fall in love again, then eros will help you to do just that. If you don't have the will, then we need to do some further work before you move on. Talk to a therapist – me! We can do some good one-to-one work to get you to a better place.

You have to choose to be willing to fall in love again with the person to whom you are married or in a relationship. You have to resolve in your mind to want to try, even if the energy is not yet there. Falling in love begins with your mind making a choice. Surrendering your choice does leave you vulnerable to being hurt, but the risk of such pain is the price for all good relationships. Relationships are risky. At times our ego needs to diminish and we build up our partner! Are you willing to pay the price?

Anger and unforgiveness will be total blocks to your ability to mend the rift. They have to be removed. Eros love is a pleasurable, but learned response. It responds to what the five senses see and detect as coming back from the other person; the way they look, feel, say things, do things and the shared emotional experiences. Consistently think on the favourable things about your relationship and have them imprinted on your mind. Banish the negative imprints of hurt from the past by choosing not to continue to churn them around in your mind and give them room to breed contempt.

Use your thought life in a constructive way. The thought life can be good and very positive and plays a very important role. Choose to think about the honourable and pleasing aspects about your partner. It is a choice. You are not a hostage to your thoughts. That is not true. Take back control.

Remember at the beginning of the union how you once felt when you held each other close. Think about those positive things that first attracted you. Look at your partner through another person's eyes and objectively assess what others may be seeing about their good qualities, which you may have lost sight of – as familiarity has bred contempt. How long has it been since your heart leapt for joy at seeing your partner. You felt like giving them a hug of appreciation for the sake of it but something stopped you! Why not just do it? Would you like to do it now? Go on then, do it! When they look at you strangely, just tell them that a therapist told you to do it!

Use your imagination to fall in love again, to renew romantic love, to keep eros love alive. Love must grow or it will die. Love coasting is love dwindling and going downhill.

Imagination is perhaps one of the strongest natural powers which we have and it must not always be seen as being negative or used in a negative manner.

HAPPY DAYS TREATS are things we can do to bring a smile to the face of our partner. We are talking of ways to keep the courtship and relationship fresh. Happy days treats are in some way sensual and so it has to be something that draws you close; such as setting the bath, with candles and scents and you getting in with your partner! a picnic; a takeaway at home - but with a twist - candles, table cloth, menus and fully dressed up as if going out to a posh restaurant!

Each partner will have one or two minutes to think of two things which will make them happy and that could be carried out by the other partner. Whatever it is you decide to do, you should perform it sufficiently frequently. After you do it on the first occasion, you should actually tell your partner that was your "Happy Days treat". Then they will know. They need to know. (I know that sounds a little unromantic)! The other person should actually acknowledge that it has been done, without any fuss. Thereafter, each time it is done, the other partner should show appreciation by simply saying "Thank you".

You are communicating value to the partner by your actions. It says that you were thinking about them. You did not leave it at just fond thoughts, but you took action. You did something. Many have good intentions, but stop at that. Be consistent in your Happy Days treats. It need not be expensive things. Habit is desirable. Habit is not always a negative word.

"Happy Days treat" is not about what you do – the act itself. It is the thought behind the act. It is a state of the mind. It is the fact that you thought about your partner when you did the exercise. Frequently it is the small things which are much more valuable than the big or expensive things. The unexpected "hello" phone call at work, particularly on a day when they know you have a very busy schedule - speaks volumes and is foreplay at work! If it is small and inexpensive then it is more likely to be done frequently.

Concentrate on the positive experiences and pleasures of the past. Day dream. You will have to give up any other attachments or figures that feature in your day dreams. Perhaps there are fantasy characters you have taken from a movie, Hollywood, TV character or from a book. Think about it. It is the way we have been nurturing our fantasy life in a wrong and inappropriate way which has set many up for cybersex with "false" intimacies. That sort of thought life is not conducive to building eros love.

A substitute person or item (perhaps a pet in whom you now channel your affections!) is not the way forward. We fill the emotional vacuum by day dreaming about someone else or something else that brings pleasure. Often because our core emotional needs are not being met. You may have built some protection around that fantasy image and be resistant and very reluctant to let them go. Has the pet taken more of your affections? We will find many ways to soothe away the pain when relationships are not working well.

You may do battle with me at this point. You are attached to your fantasy image and don't see the need to give it up. Surely you deserve the fantasy and reality and fantasy can co-exist along side each other! I suggest to you that you can only serve one master at a time. You will eventually love one and hate the other!

We have to look again at our fantasy life and ask whether it is conducive to rebuilding married life and long term relationship. Your thought life can be positive and have a positive influence on your relationship. It can be harnessed and used more constructively.

Do not allow anyone to criticise your partner in front of you, even when you may be upset or annoyed with them. Likewise be practiced and familiar with speaking only good and wholesome things about your partner to other people. Remember that your words carry authority and purpose. It has the power to build up and edify or tear down and destroy. Dwell on the positive side of your partner's character and personality. Do that consistently and watch them visibility change over time – in front of you!

You then need to provide the right emotional climate for the love to grow. It is called foreplay. Foreplay can be sensual and not always sexual in intent. It is the telephone calls at work anticipating your meeting up at home; it is the joint anticipation of a forthcoming holiday or weekend away; it is the planning of that holiday together (and not just the old practice of leaving one person to do it and you just turn up)! It is the little note in a wallet, purse or sandwich container or pockets saying "I Love You". It is sharing your time together and not separately or reducing your time spent apart and instead doing the task, hobby or sport together. Do it together periodically, even if you don't even like their hobby, sport or thing which occupies so much of their time.

Practice physically touching each other with affectionate pats or caresses in a non-sexual way. That should eventually get rid of any expectation that it must lead to sex. Use eye contact. It shows you are genuine. Work on your appearance. That T-shirt or night wear you have had for many years and is faded and discoloured from many washes should be discarded. It can speak volumes about how you regard your partner. If you would feel uncomfortable for a visitor to see you in it, then don't feel comfortable with it whilst with your partner. A bit over the top? Maybe, but we need to rebuild at a level that we want to sustain for the long run!

Just like a "Happy Days treat", a **Sexy surprise** is something that you and your partner will remember for a long time and is undertaken sufficiently frequently to add spice to life. A sexy surprise is so called because only you can make it a surprise that is sexy. It would of course be inappropriate for someone else to undertake a sexy surprise for you or your partner! Do not be afraid to go for something fully sexy as a surprise. For example, setting the bath for both of you, with bubble bath and exotic oils and floating candles, when previously you had separate baths. A bit lame that one isn't is! Can you better that?

Do not nag each other. Do not dominate each other. Encourage each other. Support each other. Undertake joint ventures rather than separate ventures where at all possible. As romantic/eros love develops, habit (which is not always a bad thing) will help to maintain a keen desire to keep working to reap the benefits you start to see appearing in the relationship. Eros is sacrificial. Is that no longer an acceptable thing to do in today's culture?

A reasoning you may put forward for avoiding romantic/eros love is that those things belonged to the early days of courtship and infatuation and therefore not for us. We have matured past such things – like holding hands. You may say that you have both matured beyond needing to do such trivial/petty romantic things; that holding hands in public is just not necessary for demonstrating affection; that belongs to the young. You may suggest that neither of you really want those sort of things in your relationship. You may suggest that you do them in other ways. But do you? Really! Check it out with your partner. Ask what they think. You may be surprised. Then you spend the time trying to persuade them that you do and identify previous occasions!

The point is that every relationship needs romantic /eros love. Ensure that you discuss with your partner all those practical endearments before you decide the relationship does not need or want them. Don't make assumptions and don't make the decision for your partner. Eros love is an essential facet of the five loves.

Chapter 12

Love me in five ways (3)

STORGE: (Security)

Storge is the third of our five loves. It is a most valuable and expensive gift. It is described as the kind of love shared by parents and children, brothers and sisters; a relationship which will always be there for you, despite being rejected by others; a safe place/haven. It is the need (which we all have) to belong or to be a part of a close knit system with people who care, are loyal and sincere. It is a relationship which provides emotional refuge from a world which can be cold, harsh, hard and uncompromisingly hostile.

Storge provides the atmosphere of security in which love is able to dwell, thrive and flourish. The absence of storge love is like a house without a roof. It is storge love which carries the relationship through the rocky years. When things seem to flounder around you, including the relationship; when push comes to shove; redundancy beckons; ill-health threatens stability; rejections which we face in life. It is because of storge love that we are confident in the relationship despite the turmoil going on around us in life. It provides assurance and comfort that our partner will always be there for us; that they are a solid rock to whom we can still turn.

We all need a place which we can call home, not just brick and mortar of four walls, but an atmosphere that is secure and we feel comfortable. Personal growth of one enhances both. Waywardness of one will likewise affect the other in some way. There is loyal support. There should be a natural affection towards each other, being warm, kind and devoted, despite seeing and knowing each other's faults.

Storge is the expression of total confidence one in the other, especially when the going is tough for one partner - perhaps in a work situation. It is the support and the being there. It is the listening, the understanding, the communicating, the sympathising and being the confidant.

When you hide your hurts and the way you are feeling from your partner, an absence of storge is self evident. Storge means a shoulder to cry on; being there at times of crises. There should be a comfortable familiarity so that partners enjoy being together and feel pleasantly at ease with each other.

Storge love is simple, down to earth and uncomplicated. It actually takes some time and consistent behaviour, to build this type of love into a relationship, where the foundations of loyalty, support and kindness are evident. Storge love does not just exist and is not there from the beginning of a relationship. It has to be built and then maintained. No one tells us that do they! It is possible to start to build this type of love so that your relationship becomes a place of homecoming – with pleasure.

You can give this gift to your partner. It is a very expensive gift; a gift of belonging. That should be your very first gift to your partner in the renewal of your re-commitment vows as you make the choice to love them with storge love.

The reasons why you originally got together, married (by choice, necessity, convenience, duress or otherwise) need not matter. They should be allowed to die a quiet death as you chose no longer to give them place of thought in your mind. You can start afresh right now and choose to love your partner.

We can learn a great deal about relationships, choices, apparent incompatibility, as well as their development from the book, stage play and film called Hobson's Choice. This is a worthwhile viewing. You hold a great deal of power to build up and transform or tear down your Partner.

In Hobson's Choice we gain a representation of how a person's life can be dramatically transformed by the other person. We see so many of the five loves being demonstrated so that you can witness what they actually look like. Insecurity, low self-esteem, and lack of belief can be radically changed by one partner in the other.

In *Hobson's Choice* you see the change as Will listened outside of Aida's mother's house and he heard what Maggie (the wife he had not planned on) was saying about him. She bolstered him up in front of others and continued to do that in the face of adversity and criticism aimed at him. She stood up for him in all situations. Observe how he grew in self-esteem.

She speaks well of him and gives a good and honestly held representation of him in front of others, particularly Mrs Hepworth (who gave them a loan to start their first business). You will see love developing; a love that was not there at the start of their courtship.

We see clear identifiable features of a good relationship portraying that will last. We see glimpses of commitment. Also an apparent or perceived roll reversal when Maggie is in the perceived role of the man by asking him out and driving the relationship. She courted him. She identified her talents and made use of them. She was able to identify the talents and qualities in him and she told him so. In telling him so, he started to believe. When he believed, he took action and those qualities showed themselves for all to see. In turn, that made her proud.

She asked him to marry her. She fights for him. She stands up for him. You have the power to build up your partner or to tear them down. You can enhance or restore their self-esteem. Note the partnership that developed within the relationship. She shows the affection. They kiss at her instigation. Yet they complement each other! Perhaps against all the odds!

Over time and as they develop (both as business partners and husband and wife), he sees the new shop sign with his name on it. That sight engendered within him a sense of pride and achievement. His self image is being transformed in front of us. Note, however, Maggie had actually risked all for him, including possible loss of her own side of the family. Observe how she deals with her in-laws outside the church prior to the wedding. He becomes more important than his brother-in-laws, who were respected business people.

Her father (for who Will had worked and greatly feared with trepidation) visits on the wedding day. She says "we are one now...". "You call him father ...". "Ask my husband if you can come in...". She gives Will authority in the relationship in front of her father! She encourages him and continues to build him up, pointing out that in a few years time he would be thought of more than his two brother-in-laws. Time proved her right!

Note the preparation for the first wedding night. Shyness is evident, but a willingness to take his place. Together they share the sight of their first income, a penny from the first sale of a pair of shoes. Observe the meeting with Will's father-in-law at the end of the film.

Now Will is even able to put an ultimatum to his father-in-law, whom he used to revere and feared. What a transformation. Will's business prowess, various other skills and self-confidence are so developed that he is now able to stand up to his father-in-law and negotiate.

You may not have loved your partner when you first got together or married. You may not actually feel in love with them right now. (Feelings do not always tell the truth – beware)! But you can choose to love again and learn how. You have the power to build up your partner to give and restore self-esteem. Those are very valuable gifts. The five loves work! Try them, but at times, maybe you will need a little help from a therapist – like me!

Chapter 13

Love me in five ways (4)

PHILEO: (Fellowship/Friendship)

Phileo is the fourth of our five loves. It is the love one feels for a cherished friend of either sex. This love is conditional and is reactive to what it sees in the other and what comes back. It is a love which cherishes and has tender affection for the beloved, but always expects a response. (This is in stark contrast to agape which we shall see does not demand a response).

Phileo is a comradeship, sharing, communication and friendship. It is dear friends who enjoy each other's closeness and companionship; sharing each other's intimate thoughts, feelings, attitudes, plans, dreams, time, interests, aspirations, as well as intimate things that would not be shared with anyone else.

Many relationships work for a lot of couples who have satisfying sexual intercourse, but lack phileo love - having a very dear friend/companion in the other person, with whom they can share everything. I know that what I am about to say will challenge well entrenched practices and not perhaps fall on receptive ears! Ladies your best friend should not be the girl friend to whom you tell most things. Guys, your best friend should not be that other male who listens to your stuff.

Neither of you in the couple relationship should have someone other than each other as your best friend! It has to change.

That other person outside the couple relationship can be a really good good friend and be the one to whom you can tell everything, where you cannot tell some things to your partner. That has to change. I know that is a tall order and is trespassing on a "no go" area. Up until now a lot of what I have been saying may have been challenging at times, but you could perhaps start to have a go, but may be what I have just suggested is simply going too too far and this is where our friendship diminishes and I will not get your endorsement from this book as a therapist!

Before you do battle with me and perhaps stop reading and throw this book down, consider the following: Could your remonstration at me and against me, parallel what you are doing to your partner and how you are treating them as you retain a best friend with pride of place in your life more so than they have?

Sometimes our very busy agenda stops phileo love. There is no time to build up this type of love within the relationship. When the children have grown up we see the reason why 25 or 35 years of relationship come to an end after the children have left home. The glue which had become a significant feature holding the status quo of the relationship in place has gone. The topic of conversation has changed. You did not know that the children leaving were the signal that you had been waiting for (unconsciously) to let go trying to live in the relationship. Relationship without fellowship/interaction is a dull relationship.

You had both long ago let the relationship drift. Life stage changes happened with age, but you stayed. Now you can see a perceived better future and a readiness to grab it; and who can blame you. The illusion still bought into is that "the grass is (and it must be!) greener on the other side"). The other one is that "there are plenty of fishes in the sea". The problem! We take our stuff (good and not so good – which has been with us from childhood) into the new relationship – unresolved. Guess what – the new partner, in time, becomes a mirror which shows up the unresolved stuff inside of up. Another casualty relationship could be breeding. We know that second and third time around marriages have an even higher fall out rate.

You say that you gave it your all; then why the guilt when you are now at liberty to leave? May be you know that you cannot say
116

with total confidence (hand on heart) that you have given it your everything. You know there is a last step you need to take. Don't fight me the messenger! Let go. Do what you know that you need to do.

This is where you will be thrown into confusion. Guilt has set in and your battle with self and me now starts.

We can make these observations about phileo. It is based on emotions and so reacts to feelings. It reacts to what we see and so reacts to the qualities of the other person. Therefore we need to change our perspective and what we think we see in the other person. We have to chose (consciously) to dwell on their positive attributes and begin to let go of those negative imprints. It is a matter of choice.

It requires reaction from the other person and interaction. It desires feedback; it wants comradeship, fellowship and communication.

Phileo does not automatically appear when the relationship commitment is given, vows are said or rings exchanged. It is strangely absent from many many relationships through neglect. Couples have lost the rapport to rebuild

phileo. Many never bother. Many never had it, even in their courting relationships. They lean too heavily on the romantic and sex, to the detriment of the other *loves*.

The absence of phileo love will show and couples try to fill the void with all sorts of things. The way to start building phileo is to start to share with each other the way you feel and your need to have a best friend as your partner. Before being lovers learn to be best friends.

Remember that the conditions you are seeking to build to grow phileo love must be conducive to a friendship. It has the very same facets and attributes. How would you develop and maintain a very very close friendship which you strongly desire? Use the same skills. You must therefore understand the dynamics of how friendships are formed and maintained. If this has not been a strong point of yours, then seek input from a therapist with whom you can do some individual work around relationships.

You need to start doing more things together. That does not necessarily mean losing your individual identity and being in each others pockets. It means that probably the relationship has been drifting, such that you both have separate pursuits. Reduce the number of social things which you do separately and do more things jointly. Sacrifice some of your hobbies/social events to be with your partner. Put yourself out to be with them as they take part in their social events/hobbies. Be supportive. Be self-sacrificing.

Show an interest as if you were trying to woo

someone to whom you were attracted before you got together. You certainly would have and did go out of your way at that time to win them and build up the relationship. Do it again.

Remember that this unilateral attempt to develop phileo love will not last for too long before resentment sets in because phileo expects a response from the other person. If that response is not quickly forthcoming – and it may well not be seen because the partner continue to live life as they always did before – then strong feelings to give up will follow. Phileo needs help from the other four loves? Is this too costly a sacrifice for you?

Communication has something to do with phileo and so we discuss it in a separate chapter as a tool and additional resource necessary for re-building phileo. Never repeat to anyone else the private things your partner shares with you without always first getting their express consent. Give your partner your total attention and listen with interest while they become more

comfortable in expressing themselves. This may be a new skill you both need time to develop. Use eye contact. Remember that it may not be easy for them to share, especially at the early stage of building phileo and learning new communication skills and practice.

Do not interrupt, pre-empt or jump to

conclusions about what is being said. Acknowledge that you understand what is said even if you do disagree. Best to repeat back to ensure that you did understand what was being said, rather than assume. You are entitled to disagree, but do not let your disagreement sound like disapproval.

Feelings of blame will cause the other person to become defensive and communication will be breaking down. When communication breaks down, rapport will need to be re-established. It is best to find something else to do and focus on for the rest of that day and move away from that particular subject matter.

Men can use the silent treatment to punish wives. The silent treatment is an effective weapon which should be banished from the relationship. The same is true of nagging each other. Women are generally more talkative and men can switch off at given points. Listening well is a valuable gift that we give to the other person, but remember to set definite time limits and stick to them.

Plan uninterrupted times and give attention to the other. Act as if you are interested and actually be interested as your partner talks. Begin to allow barriers that were erected to protect you, to come down as time goes by. Barriers are bars to effective communication. Pay particular attention to each other, especially when other people are around so that your partner knows that you recognise their presence in the midst of other people.

Phileo love, like any friendship, requires attention so that it does not die. This love can be developed between two very dissimilar people who married under extreme conditions, for whatever reasons and when love was absent. Where the two care enough for each other to want to live together and develop love, it is possible.

Plan a DVD night in the car parked up in the garage, with popcorn and afterwards - whatever takes your fancy! A candle lit dinner at home (whether it is in the form of a take-a-way or one that you cook) is complemented by an unusual style of dressing up for the occasion! Be imaginative. A massage will mostly always be a pleasing starter or after dinner treat.

The aim is to bring back romance into the Relationship. Put aside shyness. Do try hard to think of something unexpected, perhaps humorous which you can do for your partner and do it every now and then.

Chapter 14

Love me in five ways (5)

"How you think when you lose determines how long it will be until you win." — G.K. Chesterton

AGAPE: (Unconditional)

Agape is the fifth of our five loves. At some point in a relationship we may be tested harshly indeed by a crisis. Perhaps for a longer period than we could have imagined or expected we have tried to love the unlovable. We are starkly face to face with a situation of "*for better or for worse*". Unlovable traits show up in the partner. The toll on you has already been great. Yet the need in them will only be met by you continuing to express and demonstrate unconditional love. A very tall order indeed.

Agape is the totally unselfish love that has the capacity to give and keep on giving without a reciprocal return. It lacks any co-dependency attributes. We do not expect to receive back! That is just too tall an order.

Unconditional love is the greatest gift children give to their parents. They love no matter what.

Many of us do not have this quality and therefore without doubt we are moving from the physical to a spiritual quality. It is a quality which we may not have and need from a higher power and authority. I and others chose to call that higher power – God.

Here is what Agape looks like. It values. It serves. It continues without receiving back; without a thank you; without an acknowledgement. It has the attributes of grace and unconditional forgiveness. The cost is challenging indeed. Are you ready yet to call a truce on the past?

Agape love is of particular significance to those partners who are trying desperately to save their relationship; where the love has gone and love definitely does not seem to live here anymore. Love may have gone many years ago – at least from one party. Yet one is determined to hold on, seeing a glimmer of hope to rebuild the relationship. Separation is beckoning or has happened. Divorce is a next inevitable step.

Agape is an exercise of choice and not dependent upon feelings. You choose to love with agape love or choose not to. If you choose not to, then what is said after this point about agape love will sound impossible, unreasonable, belittling and slavery. It will not connect or resonate with you. It will be an absolute turn off and a feeling of derision for anyone who would stoop so low for another person! Get a life - might be your sentiment.

Agape love focuses on what you know is right rather than on feelings. At times (and there will be many such times during the endeavours) feelings have to be overridden. Feelings do not always tell the truth. You do and say things even though you do not feel like doing or saying those things. – with a focused purpose of winning the other back into the relationship.

A relationship possessing agape love can survive anything. It is agape that keeps the relationship going when the natural love falters or dies. Even the most natural love will end eventually when there is no response. Agape keeps on going. It is the supernatural which comes from God which helps and renews your capacity to stay in there. Just like 12 step programmes, you gain tenacity from somewhere, including your support network of best friends, who are there for you as allies.

It is so important that we bear in mind that our relationship example is something from which our children will be taking note. We are teaching our children by example. They will learn about love and relationship (rightly or wrongly) from what they observe in us. That is how we first learnt how to do relationships! Children will feel insecurity if they cannot count on the love that mother has for father and the love that father has for mother.

Children have a right for their parents to love each other and for their parents to provide security for the children. They have a right to firm foundations within the home. We live in a culture of rights and enforcement of rights.

124

Children have an inalienable right to grow up with a mother and father. It is their right. The price paid for growing up with insecurity is immense and we therapists will witness to that fact. So often there are repeated broken relationships which seem to follow the same person.

Agape love is always concerned with doing what is best for the beloved. It is right that as we look at agape love we ask, is it really achievable and at what price? At what price to our self respect when we see no response from the

other partner. A post modern society would not accept this type of teaching; to give and keep on giving, even if you see yourself as the wronged party. It is contrary to the world's system.

That is why I again urge you to take some time to contemplate the full extent of what agape love really means so that you will understand that there will be a price to pay for trying to implement it, but potentially a wonderful reward.

"Music... will help dissolve your perplexities and purify your character and sensibilities, and in time of care and sorrow, will keep a fountain of joy alive in you."
— *Dietrich Bonhoeffer*

Agape love will enhance your partner's self image. The better a person feels about them self the better they will be able to function within the relationship. Someone who feels love all the time, knowing it is not based on their own performance, feels uniquely valued as a person. The hot coals heaped on them cannot but command a response.

Unconditional love needs to become a habit. When it becomes a habit then it can carry your partner through periods of severe stress. The ultimate purpose is to win the other person back into the relationship. Agape is love in action, not just good intentions. Agape love will very often clash head on with old learned habits - which come from a world view that loving must be conditional.

What I am not condoning is an abused person remaining in an abusive relationship. It is not acceptable for either party to experience emotional, physical or spiritual abuse of any form and to live in or remain in such a situation. Get help. Please.

Separateness becomes necessary in order to protect self. Getting back together can only occur after professional help – in the form of treatment. Treatment is always a prerequisite to parties getting back together.

Change your focus

I caution not to use agape with the intention of reforming or changing your partner! That is not agape at work. That is another form of conditional love. Accept them as they are. First seek to change your own behaviour and you will see what happens next.

Some say there are no difficult people only limitations on our ability to deal with certain individuals! They will also say there are no irritable people only limitations on our ability to understand why certain people behave the way they do! To change the way others behave, the most effective tool we have is our own behaviour. The more flexible we are, the more able we are to influence others. In order to change own behaviour people need to feel safe, appreciated and understood. That provides an impetus for change.

Maybe people are not the problem. It is the problem which is the problem. Change your focus from the person to the problem. Do that by standing outside the problem. See the problem, not the person as the problem. The person is not the problem. The problem is the problem. Externalising the problem in this way is something we can do some work around in therapy.

"In normal life we hardly realize how much more we receive than we give, and life cannot be rich without such gratitude. It is so easy to overestimate the importance of our own achievements compared with what we owe to the help of others."
— *Dietrich Bonhoeffer*

Chapter 15

When the 5 loves disappear

In the film Shirley Valentine, we see a typical example of what happens when, over time, a relationship is coasting. Like a coasting car, it must likewise be going downhill – since nothing can coast on a level surface or on its way up!

There is a lot of Shirley Valentine in many of our relationships. We all need to feel appreciated.

We are vulnerable to cheating on our partner - because of loneliness; because of the feeling of not being appreciated; because someone seems to understand us better than our partner. That is what happens when we choose flight. We move away from where our needs are not being met to a place where we feel they can be met, but that often puts us in a vulnerable place.

That initially attentive ear may belong to someone who is also in need of what you have to offer for their listening ear. "You understand me so much better than my partner – that is why I like to spend time with you" – has a kick back at a point. Misapplied affection comes to light with a vengeance after the sex is done. Reality sets in and you realise that you fell for the emotions of the feelings you got being with the third person. They no longer fill that void which being with them initially seem to do.

Shirley Valentine had endured life with her husband and when opportunity presented for flight she literally did so! The character called Costa was able to seduce her as she longed again for the feeling of being in love. How? He did it in a number of ways. First, he is a very good listener. Then he enhanced her fantasy. He helped her to discover herself. Actually, he did not have to do very much, but little was definitely much in this instance.

Observe these things other traits about Costas. He has some good hearing and listening skills, including eye contact as he let her just talk. He is a charmer. He knows how to dream and join Shirley in her dreams. He knows how to turn her negatives into positives.

He nearly seduces her, but she comes to a realisation that what she pines for and misses is not another man, but she has fallen in love with the idea of being alive; especially so when she is with him. The stage is set for a man to romance her and sweep her off her feet.

Shirley's husband is frightened of anything that is different. He comes to a realisation that he is boring. Reference is made to him coming home one day with a smile on his face and his wife did not recognise him! His son is able to remind him how he once laughed and talked and now how boring he had become.

If you are able to obtain the DVD, watch it and then you may care to answer or reflect on your thoughts about the answers to the following questions:

What is going on for Shirley when she says the following?:

"When you've imagined something...it never turns out like that...you land up feeling pretty daft and awfully old."

"You can't bring logic into this – this is relationship."

"Relationship is like the Middle East – there is no solution"

"Where is Shirley Valentine? She got lost in all this unused life"

"Sex is like supermarkets – just a lot of pushing and shoving and you still come out with very little".

One of those five loves which we looked at was Agape. Identify your own need and in order to get those needs met, love the other person consistently over the next 6 months using a language of love that they understand. The aim is not to change the other person, but to start to enjoy life more by doing things which bring benefit to them. That "giving heart" (or sacrificial) approach will see you getting your needs met in the fullness of time.

In an affair situation, a man might blame the woman for not taking care of his physical and sexual needs. The woman might blame the man for working too many long hours and not being there for her. They both focus on the other's failings rather than on what each needs to change within themself. Don't look to the other person to make you happy. It is not about "you scratch my back and I'll scratch yours". That formula has the perception of working for some couples, but in truth IT DOES NOT WORK. Don't look to the other person to meet your emotional needs. You set them up to fail.

We tend to look for other people to meet us half way. Our happiness and well-being are not in the hands of the other person. We buy into a lie. It is a myth. People will fail us at some point. Abraham Lincoln said "I reckon that people are about as happy as they make up their minds to be".

Maybe we need to grow up - using the language of Transactional Analysis! Otherwise known as TA, it is a tool we shall look at. In TA language, an Adult is a person capable of responsibility for self. A person who is capable of such responsibility, but does not accept full responsibility, must be functioning as a Child. A child is someone that remains dependant on others and blames others. An adult is no longer a child, so start the transition into adulthood now. Involve a trusted friend. Give them permission to speak into your situation when they see you not taking your own responsibility. Have some counselling.

Your motto could be this: "I have to be the best that I can be, so that I can give the best that I am, so that you can be the best that you can be".

Chapter 16

Communication or miscommunication? (1)

"The most basic of all human needs is the need to understand and be understood. The best way to understand people is to listen to them."
— Ralph Nichols

Enhancing communication skills

There is a difference between Men & Women! She talks about the last six months of courtship and how it was for her. She is anxious about the next six months and desires that it develops well. She wants to discuss with him whether there is something more or different that she should do.

She chooses to have the conversation after a lovely restaurant meal and they are driving back to her house. He is thinking about an engine noise coming from the bonnet of the car he purchased just two days ago and is listening intently to that noise as she is talking passionately about their growth! They are missing each other's topics of conversation, but neither yet realizes that they are on totally different subject matters and very different headspace! Sound familiar?

Picture the scene of the fifty-something year old couple having a weekend break in a nice hotel. Their children have long since left home. The couple goes down for dinner in the restaurant where there are a number of couples of similar and older ages. Apart from some quiet background music and the clatter of cutlery, there is very little sound. There is not very much chatter and certainly none between our couple.

They have very little to say to each other, other than the occasional glance or a request to pass the salt. Long ago they lost the art of conversation. Their topic of conversation was only ever about the children and the children have now left home. They find themselves without sufficient subject matter to keep a conversation going between them. Marital dullness is not confined to middle and later years.

Communication is like a bicycle wheel. Picture the two of you riding along the road to your destination, but not getting very far because both wheels on your tandem bicycle are buckled. You will get to your destination, but not very fast and it is taking more effort to cover the distance.

Now let's remove one of the bicycle wheels and take a look at what we have in front of us. We can view the hub in the middle and call it "communication". The hub needs to be tight and work well, because attached to it are the spokes. The spokes are various life issues that we all face. Life will throw up lots of stuff that we have to deal with. Those spokes or life issues can be negotiated around and got over much better by the two of you where the hub (communication) is tight and working well for the two of you. How do we tighten the hub so that it keeps the spokes tightly attached to it and stop the wheel warping and hindering progress?

The intention is to tighten up the hub so that when communication is working much better for the two of you, both of you can better tackle life issues. Let us look at the features of Communication. It includes body posture, gestures (such as head nods), facial expression, eye contact, physical proximity, appearance, style of speech, tone and volume of voice, words (and the different meanings they may have to you) and physical contact (such as hand shakes). Remember cultural differences and word nuances!

The intention is that when therapy comes to an end, armed with new communication skills each is better equipped to tackle those spoke issues which life will continue to throw up. Improved communication skill is a life skill which works in the home, work, gym or wherever interaction with another takes place.

Most of the time we do not check out that we have understood what the other has endeavoured to communicate. We all have communication filters. Stuff happens to us in life. The stuff results in life experiences. Some of that stuff may have hurt us and those experiences are remembered. The brain remembers those experiences and will cause us to put in place barriers to avoid repetition of hurt.

We might call those hurts baggage or just issues. We have inside of us good and not so good stuff from experiences. Some serve us well for a season but life changes. We go through life stages. Relationships change. The same stuff may no longer serve us well in different seasons or in new relationships, even though we are doing life the same way as before. It just is not working well any more. Why not?

When we are communicating, the information is passing through the filters that we have. We all have filters. The message being transmitted is going through the receiver but the receiver has filters and that means the message can come out the other end looking very different to what went in and was received.

For there to be effective transmission and receipt, the equipment must be working well. Stress, headaches, worry, multi-tasking and distractions are some things which act as blocks to effective transmission. We need to learn to listen effectively and hear well. The speaker must have a clear idea of what they intend to communicate.

The recipient must feel the message is relevant and be interested or greater levels of concentration will be required. The time and place must be appropriate. Both should be free from interference from emotions and past history. They must share the same language and not have coded meanings.

The problem we have is that on a lot of occasions many of those things are not present and so there are problems in transmitting and/or receiving. Filters may act as blocks. What is said is not what we want to hear and so we do not listen or we do not interpret it the way it was intended. That can all be happening consciously or even unconsciously. It is the unconscious which is perhaps more difficult to identify and deal with.

Don't be entrenched and fixed in your views. Don't be dogmatic. Leave scope for a different opinion. I demonstrate this in therapy by showing ambiguous picture shapes and ask each person to describe what they see. Some cannot see all the different images contained in one picture. They need help. When pointed out, they exclaim with pleasure that they too can now see the differing images! But they needed help. Until they received help, many will hold firmly to their view that there is nothing further to be seen.

Life is not always Black and White. Sometimes we all need help to see and better understand that which we just cannot see or understand with our own five senses. Sometimes we need someone to help us introduce some colour into our black and white, all or nothing way of thinking. That so often is all that counselling is about!

Allow room for someone else to speak into your situation rather than feel that they have nothing to say on the matter. Don't close people down constantly by your approach in conversations with them so that on the occasion when they could have voiced a view and helped you out of a scenario, they withhold. You then lose out. But you won't always know that you are losing out!

Do we do that to people including our partner? Maybe a superior attitude, long ago, set in and we cannot and do not, see it. Friends would not dare to point out such traits in us! You may not recognize or value people who may have the key to particular situations in your lives. We none of us are islands. We all need a helping hand from time to time. That is not a sign of weakness. It is recognition of a facet of healthy relationships.

Sometimes we need to think outside of the box. But often we need a little help to see how we restrict our own thinking!

9 Dots

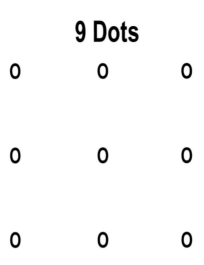

Rules: Draw 4 straight and continuous lines which must cross through each dot at least once without removing pen from paper.

Sometimes we cannot see it. Sometimes we need some help to see it. Sometimes the constraints are self imposed. Just like the ambiguous pictures we looked at. Sometimes we need to remove the shackles from our own minds so that we can think outside of the box.

If we can change our mind, then we can change our lives. But before then we need to examine what is already in and going into our heart for change to be long lasting.

Chapter 17

Communication or Miscommunication? (2)

"A friend asks, "Tell me one word which is significant in any kinds of relationship." Another friend says, "LISTEN!" — <u>*Santosh Kalwar*</u>

Enhancing Effective Communication

When we first meet someone we form a very strong impression of them within the first 40 seconds. We form a lasting opinion of them within the first 4 minutes. Our opinion will influence the way in which we respond and behave towards that person until something happens to cause us to change our mind. Even then, changing our mind is a process and is not immediate.

Our voice and body language communicate about 93% of our message. Let's break that down a bit more. Dependent upon the statistics that you read, anything from 55% to 70% of what is communicated and we take in is what we gain visually, using our sight. In other words what we see. 38% comes from what we hear (tone, pitch of voice etc) and only 7% comes from the actual words that we hear. Remember words are ambiguous.

Since *Men are from Mars and Women are from Venus* (book by John Gray); *Men don't listen and women cannot read maps* (book by Allan & Barbara Pease); that means that male and females may have varying interpretation for different words that are used.

The way someone dresses influences opinion. As a speaker, if I dress in a way that is insensitive, inappropriate or is causing you to pay more attention to it; perhaps I have been culturally insensitive in my dress sense; then for quite a long time you will have been absorbed with that fact. You will have stopped listening effectively and be distracted in your thoughts, although you will have been "hearing" noise coming out of my mouth. There is a great difference between listening and hearing.

If you detect a nervous disposition from me as I am speaking to you, my nervous disposition and shaking hands will be giving you mixed messages and reduce the impact of what I am saying. What is the importance of all of this?

It is important to maximise that which takes in most of the information whilst we communicate. That is the visual. Therefore, avoid having those important conversations sitting side by side, particularly with the television on. Text messages can be disastrous when dealing with important matters. Laying side by side and pillow talk conversations can become problematic if the subject has more importance to one of you than realised by the other. I am not saying not to do it, but I want you to be aware that the aim should be to maximise eye to eye and body to body visual contact.

That means sitting sufficiently close enough to each other in a quarter to three or perhaps a ten to two position so that you can occasionally see the whites of each other's eyes and the full body! Sitting behind a table hides a lot of body messages. The body communicates a lot of visual impressions and may be communicating a very different message to what is being voiced. It is important to read body posture signals.

We can teach our brains to say the right things, but our heart can betray us. In other words, whilst we are saying what we have rehearsed in our minds, our body language could be giving off a very different impression and contradict our spoken words! If, in truth, we were too tired for a particular conversation, but did not own up to that fact, we continue at out peril! The other person is likely to detect that we are not really listening and feel devalued.

You know those times when we encourage each other to keep speaking whilst we are washing up or doing a particular task and we tell them that we are listening whilst multi-tasking. Dangerous! We cannot give each other effective quality listening time whilst we are doing something else. If we keep doing that over time then we devalue the other person. When we feel somebody is not listening to us we feel devalued.

When we repeatedly devalue the other person they will start to lose some of those core emotional needs and then we see fight and/or flight start to come out as they seek to get those needs met.

Chapter 18

Communication or Miscommunication? (3)

"Being heard is so close to being loved that for the average person, they are almost indistinguishable." — David Augsburger

Difference between "Hearing" and "Listening"

Listening effectively is a gift. It is costly. It values the other person. It is learned and must be practiced. There is a difference between hearing and listening. You can hear my voice but where you have been concentrating for quite a few hours, from time to time, you will have stopped listening to me. Listening means that the information stops in the brain and is processed and digested. When information is not digested, then you will find you did not really listen to it and take it in and it quickly is forgotten.

Listening More Effectively

Five types of poor listeners:

1. The advisor: instead of seeking to understand and empathise, will

> want to sort out the problem by proposing a fix it. Sometimes the person who has spoken, only wanted to be heard and listened to without a solution. We men can struggle with

that. What – no advice wanted!

2. The interrupter: whilst a person is speaking they are already working

> out a reply. Whilst the brain is working out the reply they are not truly listening. Sometimes we are not aware that we interrupt each other.

3. The reasurer: is a person who perhaps interrupts prematurely and gives advice that may be little what has been said. For example, "It'll be OK".

4. The rationaliser: that person focuses on explaining why the other feels the way they do. The replies may actually totally miss the point.

5. The deflector: perhaps feels uncomfortable with the subject matter and instead of commenting on the issue, moves the conversation off into a different arena. Often ends up talking more about them self.

Good and bad time to have an important discussion

We need to recognise that at different times of the day, we each of us may be in a different place, affecting our capacity to give quality listening time. It may be late at night for one of us and not for the other or early in the morning. We therefore need to check out

145

with the other person whether "now is a good time" for them.

The 48 Hour Rule

If one of you voices to the other that "now is not a good time" for you to have a particular conversation, then you have ownership of the conversation. In other words, it is for you to go back to the other person (1 hour, 2 hours or longer, but up to a maximum of 24 hours later) and apologise to them that you were not able to have that conversation that they wanted to have. Explain that now is good for you and especially ask whether now a good time for them also.

You are respecting them and valuing them by checking out that just because you are in a better place to have the conversation, is it also a good time for them. That is giving them the right to say it is not a good time now for them. If they are not able to, then you retain ownership for a second occasion to go back to them (and that could be half an hour, 1 hour, 2 hours later, up to a maximum of a further 24 hours). In other words, twice within a period of 48 hours.

If on the second occasion it is still not convenient for that person, then you let go of the conversation. It was not your desire to have the conversation in the first place and if they want to have it, it is for them to come back to you. Realise what could happen, if we do not set some limits. Tit-for-tat could set in where they repeatedly maintain that it is not convenient for them.

Remember, that it is actually quite hard to let somebody off the hook from having a conversation which you want to have. You may have been thinking about the particular subject matter for some time and have worked it out in your mind and then you are ready to have that conversation and the other person says "now is not a good time for me"! You might feel anxious, put out and frustrated by them for not wanting to have the conversation. That will hurt. It can feel like being cut off at the knee!

Think about it and be ready for that possibility. They may not have the topic uppermost in their mind and have had a very different day to you. They must take ownership and responsibility for themself and where they are at. It can be quite a painful experience. Be prepared.

Some people may abuse the process and use it as a way to avoid discussing the subject. I would encourage you not to challenge somebody about whether they feel up to the conversation or not. Remember, it is their responsibility to come back to you twice within 48 hours.

If someone is not at a good place to give you effective listening time, then it is better not to force them to try to listen to you because the body will start to show that they are not listening to you and you will start to feel devalued. When you feel devalued over a period of time, then annoyance and fight or flight will set in.

Set Time Limits for Conversations

It is important to try to agree some time limits before you commence a particular discussion. Stick to time limits and take a break. Probably do not have a discussion for longer than 1 hour. If you have not finished the conversation, then do not agree to extend the time and just continue. Rather, agree to take a definite break, for at least 20 minutes or so, to refresh and then agree the length of time you will continue on the second occasion and stick to it. Breaks are really important even if you think you do not need them.

The Floor Card Exercise

Let's look at an effective hearing and listening skill exercise:

Think about a conversation (not a controversial one) that you may have had in the last 2 months and which you can role play again. Agree with each other that you will not hold each other to anything that is said during this role play session, because it is just that – a role play! Whoever is going to start the conversation picks up an item, such as a card, a pen, a pencil or something near at hand in the home (but not something that can cause injury!). Whoever has the object has the floor and the right to speak. Let's call that person (A) and the person without the item is (B).

(A) should invite (B) to have a conversation by first of all giving them just a short single sentence description of what the subject is about, so that the other person can decide whether they are ready to have that type of conversation or not.   Agree to have the conversation. (A) speaks a few sentences only. Remember that (B) will need to summarise what is said and so keep it manageable. Remember, a summary should be shorter!

(A) should then give feedback to (B) by saying "yes or yes, that is mostly it". If not quite right or complete, then be kind by repeating any information which they did not get right. (B) must summarise that corrected information before adding anything else. You only move on by giving more information when you feel comfortable that the other person has summarised back the previous information correctly.

I sometimes describe it as slow motion tennis. One person hits the ball across the net and before the other one hits it back they shout to that persons to ask them if they are ready. Only when they hear an affirmation, do they then hit it back. When the other person has it, before they hit it back they ask the other person if they are ready and only when they say yes, do they hit the ball back!

You cannot give the summary back if you have not been listening and only hearing! Try it and see. When we think about it, it is madness that we speak to someone and assume they have heard and understood the matter exactly as we have said it to them, without checking it out with them. That is all the floor card exercise is doing, checking out that the other person has understood what we have said at each stage, before we build the conversation. That ensures that whilst we are building the conversation we are taking the other person with us. Many times conversations go off at a tangent and we never actually find out why.

Those innocent discussions start out well enough, but we never find out why it has ended up quite heated and alienated us. What went wrong? Perhaps misunderstanding or misinterpretation.

Practice makes perfect, but you may hit resistance to learning a new skill and avoid trying the floor card exercise, giving various reasons. You may want to stay with or fall back on the way you previously did communication. Recognise resistance and confront it. Let me show you what resistance looks like.

Try the Signature exercise:

Find a scrap piece of paper and write your normal signature twice. Then put the pen in the other hand and do your signature twice.

Think about the process of signing with your usual dominant hand. Then consider the emotions and how you felt using your non-dominant hand.

Typically you will say that the non-dominant hand felt slower, more difficult and challenging and took more concentration.

Arm folding exercise

Let's reinforce that by trying the arm folding exercise. Fold your arms normally. Then unfold them and fold them with the other arm on top.

What was happening in both exercises? The brain had to learn a new way of doing things. It will resist change and need time to adapt. Add the fact of conflict and perhaps tension between the two of you and you will understand another reason why you may resist trying and continuing with the floor card exercise above. After all you could be setting yourselves up for potential disaster! You could also have embarked on your most significant piece of learning which will serve you well for a life time.

Just like learning to ride a bike or learning to play a new instrument, it will require repeated practice. Investment in practice will reap rewards.

Transactional Analysis, Personality Types and Ego States

Understand the person and you begin to understand what causes or contributes to conflicts. A little insight into Personality or psychological types (as a theory that explains some of the differences in people's behaviors) can prove useful. There are predictable differences in individuals which show by the different ways in which they use their minds.

We have preferences. We instinctively pick up a pen and sign our names with one preferred hand. When we fold our arms we instinctively put the right arm on top of the left or vice versa. We can use the other arm, although it will be more awkward, take more thought and effort and be slower. I touch upon a few concepts below only to sow them in your mind, but I realise that they are not developed adequately as tools for you to yet use effectively. I make them available for your own further reading around the topics.

Personality type preference is about the way an individual chooses to use the mind to **"perceive"**, **"judge"**, for **"introversion"** or for **"extraversion"**. A basic level of understanding will empower us to consider adapting our behaviour accordingly, to affect the conflict for good or bad. Just be aware of these even though I do not use space here to develop them further at this time.

Transactional Analysis (TA) also explains

and categorises the way a person relates or behaves. Their behaviour may differ in various circumstances and situations as they adopt different ego states. A person's ego state includes their thoughts, behaviours and feelings and they express them in three different ways. They are **Parent, Adult** or **Child**. TA is about analysing the mechanics which operate when people endeavour to communicate their thoughts, feelings and behaviour. As a tool, it provides insight into managing and resolving conflicts. It is a useful tool in communication skills.

Whilst in the **Parent** state we express thoughts, feelings and behaviours learned from our parent figures – which were nurturing and protecting of us. They are the values and morals from our parents and are visible when we are critical and Judgmental; shown for example, by wagging the finger in a stern rebuke in a parental disciplinarian manner. In the **Adult** state those behaviours, thoughts and feelings are when we are more likely to make rational decisions and deal appropriately with options. Here we are rational with the facts and unemotional in problem solving or decision-making. The **Child** state is a free spirit wanting to have fun, be carefree and without responsibility. We experience the emotions from childhood. We use them to get our way.

An example, is where an Assistant solicitor says to the trainee, "*My boss is not going to be pleased with your piece of research and I'll*
153

be in for it if I give that to him, because you have missed out a vital piece of information".

Concerned about his standing with the partner, the Assistant solicitor is in a dependent child ego state with the Trainee. The trainee may reply, "*No problem, I'll find the missing information and include it promptly for you. Don't worry.*" The trainee is in the parent (reassuring) ego state.

The importance of these concepts is that knowledge of their dynamics can enable us to break out, break free and change as circumstances require. Realisation about potential choices can enable us to stop, think and change our method of communication and thereby affect the relationship. So often, we see examples of how a person we are in contact with seems to make us behave in a particular way and we do not know why! We wish we could be set free.

Conflicts are difficult to solve until parties face up to the realities of the situation. That may be a painful process and can only come about when the individual is behaving in their Adult ego state and recognise all the facts and implications surrounding their course of action.

We may not always have or know the full facts. Allow for difference and a different perspective. What we think we see and know may not be the full picture!! Remember the ambiguous pictures.

Chapter 19

A Life time love affair. A tall order or realistic?

"It sounded an excellent plan, no doubt, and very neatly and simply arranged

The only difficulty was, that she had not the smallest idea how to set about it...."

(Alice in Wonderland, Lewis Carroll)

The key is consistent and regular intimacy. Ideally the intimacy building process should begin with the newly weds. Pre-relationship/marriage preparation sessions should be an essential necessity. For many, their happiness in relationships depends on how well their partner performs. That is a tall order to live up to and will therefore frequently end in failure.

Few things are as important as the health of your relationship. Build an intimate relationship. Courtship begins the laying down and building the foundations. Partners should be team and soul mates, yoked together in a common purpose. Becoming team mates takes time. Every team needs time to build, bind and grow together. Strong relationships are vital and crucial components for a healthy society.

Physical touching is a pre-requisite to intimacy. The problem is that as we progressed out of childhood we frequently did not learn how to separate physical touch and caresses (which every one of us need) from sexual connotations. We do need to cuddle, snuggle together, hug, hold hands and sit close to each other, whenever the occasion arises, without it being an expression of sex. We need warmth, reassurance and intimacy of non-sexual touching, whether we are conscious of it or not. Many have turned to sex as a substitute for the loving closeness which they yearn. We may need to unlearn some of our habits.

If you say that you are not an affectionate person or find it difficult to show affection, then the question is are you willing to learn? You actually can learn as long as you have the motivation and desire.

Remember to praise your partner. Praise is very powerful. Criticism is destructive. It puts emotional distance between you.

You will both need to recognise times when your behaviour is less than loving and you need to learn to apologise. Become familiar with apologising. Shame the devil and do it differently to what your desire tells you to do! Begin to develop more of a giving heart, rather than a taking mentality. The rewards are immense.

Why not turn to your partner right now and say "I am sorry". I give you permission to do so, even if it is mechanical! Apologising and forgiving are learned responses and are not spontaneous. It is an art. Start to practice it now.

Intimacy requires blending of the five loves. It does not just happen. There are many hindrances. You need to make time. Just do it – because you know it is right. Willingness and desire can follow later. Even if relationships are made in heaven, maintenance of them certainly occurs in an earthly setting!

Intimacy will cause you to stay in love. Without it one or both of you may be strongly tempted to seek it elsewhere and sometimes even assume the other does not want very much intimacy. Love can begin to die.

"*Shirley Valentine*" is a picture of the absence of the five loves and what happens to a couple when those loves have been absent for some time. "*Hobsons Choice*" is a representation of the five loves at work. There is, however, a book which is the most romantic piece of literature containing truths which transcends time, cultures, classes and experiences and which was written many hundreds of years ago. It contains timeless truths. It is hot! It is speaks unapologetically about relationship and sex; techniques, roles, things that can go wrong, pride, forgiveness and making up and unbridled, unrestricted passion to excess. It is a book called "Song of Solomon".

The challenge to you now is to take first

steps. Make a start. You can do it. Bite off small portions, but make a start. I am here if you need help.

Gary McFarlane BA, LLM

Gary is a Relate trained and experienced Relationship counsellor, Mediator and undertakes Sex Therapy & Sex Addiction treatment all of which are undertaken by Skype, telephone and face to face with clients from all parts of the country. He is also a member of BACP and the Association for the Treatment of Sexual Addiction & Compulsivity. Gary has been a Solicitor (now non-practising) for 22 years.

gary.g.mcfarlane@blueyonder.co.uk

www.garymcfarlane.com or

www.sexaddictiontreatment.co.uk

Tel: 0786 609 7247